D0178090

A CRASH COURSE

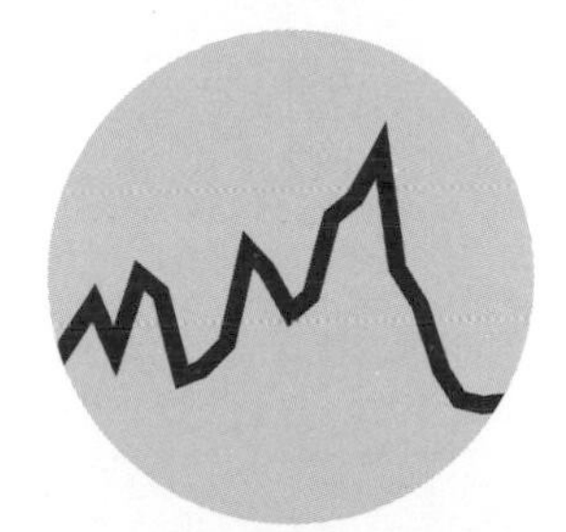

ECONOMICS

A CRASH COURSE

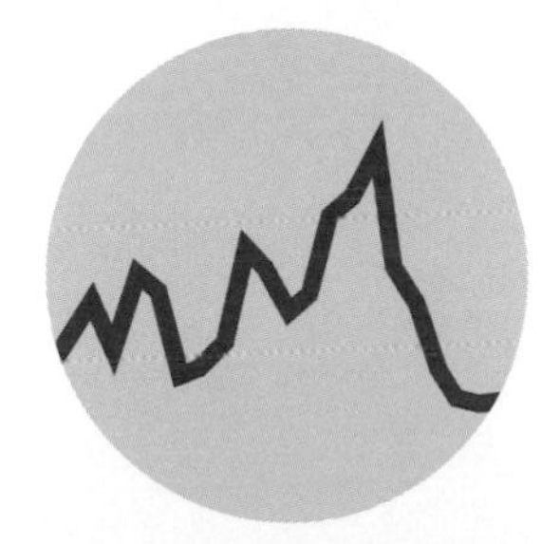

ECONOMICS

DAVID BOYLE & ANDREW SIMMS

IVY PRESS

First published in the UK in 2019 by
Ivy Press
An imprint of The Quarto Group
The Old Brewery, 6 Blundell Street
London N7 9BH, United Kingdom
T (0)20 7700 6700 **F** (0)20 7700 8066
www.QuartoKnows.com

British Library Cataloguing-in-Publication Data
A catalogue record for this book is available from the British Library

ISBN: 978-1-78240-861-1

This book was conceived, designed and produced by
Ivy Press
58 West Street, Brighton BN1 2RA, United Kingdom

Publisher Susan Kelly
Editorial Director Tom Kitch
Art Director James Lawrence
Project Editor Angela Koo
Design JC Lanaway
Illustrators Beady Eyes
Design Manager Anna Stevens
Visual Concepts Paul Carslake
Series Concept Design Michael Whitehead

Printed in China

10 9 8 7 6 5 4 3 2 1

I TRODUCTIO

Something has happened to economics recently. There was a time, not long ago, when economic ideas were a generally agreed, though narrow, set of principles. Then the continuing boom-and-bust cycle—and one spectacular bust, in the form of the financial crisis of 2007–8—combined with the failure of the best economic minds to ensure that prosperity spreads down through the economy as it is supposed to, has left a series of very obvious question marks. Suddenly, mainstream economics no longer seems quite so mainstream: from inside and outside the profession, a number of challenges and challengers have emerged, and especially from the so-called heterodox economists, who regard economics as part of a wider set of information that can be gleaned from the study of psychology, biology, and other disciplines. It now seems clear that, in search of a better understanding of how the world works, human beings and the planet have to be brought into the analysis. That is why we have structured this book in the way that we have—so that it covers the main economic ideas and history, then looks at some of the new directions that economics now seems to be heading in.

Past, present, and future

This book's 52 topics intermesh in many ways, even if they are not entirely interchangeable. There are historical topics that might have slotted into any of the four chapters, for example, just as there are timelines that show how the debate has developed over the century. We regard economics as the story of a sometimes raucous conversation about prosperity and how to achieve it. The hope is that this slim volume will provide a new generation with a good grounding in the history of economics, and in such a way that they grasp the emerging debates as they unfold.

The first chapter—Economic History—goes right back to the debate (a more recent conversation, in fact) about stone age economics and the purposes for which money was originally invented—was it to facilitate trade, or did it originally have a more ceremonial function? The jury remains out on this and on so many of the other debates in this book. Generally speaking, the ideas in the history chapter are there because they are either fundamental to understanding economics in any period, or because they appear as a critical memory because they are now archaic as far as mainstream economics is concerned—like the medieval concept of the "just price."

Although it disappeared from mainstream economics some time around the Reformation, the just price still exists in the background of economic debate—either explicitly, because people are campaigning against business behavior that previous centuries would have dubbed usurious, or because morality still lies behind so much modern economic discussion, and the way the world argues will always reflect this.

The elements of the Big Ideas chapter that follow are clearer. They are designed to build up a picture of the key ideas that have driven economics from the dawn of economic thinking, and which are likely to survive in some form or other into the future.

The third chapter—Economics and People—is more heterodox in its basic understanding. It derives from the various strands of modern economics that regard the discipline not as a set of truths unconnected with other elements of reality, but as a subset of the proper study of mankind, deriving insights into the way that money and economics works from the way that people actually behave. Such ideas remain controversial, and they challenge the general assumptions that young economists are encouraged to make. Is it true, for example, that people maximize their "utility" in every decision? Well, yes it is, but it depends how widely you define utility. Do people really spend more time shopping for themselves than they do for others? Probably not, and not even economists really believe this, but it sometimes suits them to assume it, because that is the "model" of the world they use.

It is also in this chapter that we cover some of the insights of feminist economics, especially the pioneering work by the former New Zealand MP Marilyn Waring, which has so changed the terms of debate, and in deference to which we have set out (almost) the same number of biographies dedicated to women as to men.

The final chapter—Economics and the Planet—covers some of the economic insights that have come from those whose expertise has been biological or environmental. That does not mean that the economics edge has to be excluded, just that the debate about money and prosperity needs to be seen through a lens of what is possible, given that the planet may be close to some of the limits of its sustainable renewing power. We make no apology for broadening the boundaries of economic debate in this way—the study of money and its behavior requires insights from other disciplines in order to formulate new arguments and insights.

The straitjacket of economic orthodoxy

We publish this book at a unique moment in the economics story. The "post-autistic economics" student protest in the 1990s, and the "new economics" movement that preceeded it in the 1980s, marked the first exchanges in a long-running argument at the heart of the economics establishment. In the UK, it began to gather momentum with agitation by Manchester University economics students to find ways to understand why mainstream economists had failed to predict the 2007–8 financial crisis. Students have been at the heart of this agitation ever since.

Economics as a discipline has been trying to free itself from a puritanical straitjacket of rigorously one-sided thinking. All big ideas in any discipline tend to become controlled and over-controlling in the end, and over-rationalized. This tends in turn to lead to narrow, sometimes puritanical, thinking. Over recent decades, economic orthodoxy has slowly managed to excise economic history—and with it, the study of alternative roads not taken. History and predictions, the past and the future, were rendered irrelevant to the specific issue of what needed to be done now to free up markets.

The inability of orthodoxy to predict the 2007–8 crash was just one element in the crisis of mainstream economics, and it has forced a measure of thoughtful reform. The other has been the failure of orthodox economic policy to improve the incomes of more than a handful of the richest. It wasn't what was supposed to happen.

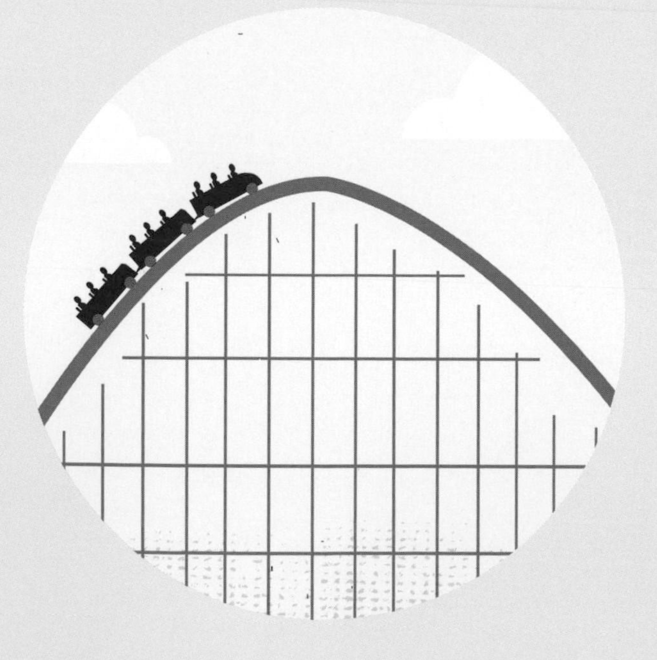

The masters of economics were always bigger than their theories. For example, American economist Milton Friedman's idea of permanent income—which explains that governments cannot rely on brief, temporary stimuli to change people's economic behavior, mainly because they will save (not spend) extra income until they are reasonably sure it will be permanent—is an example of a wider theory deriving from the way people actually behave, not the way that economic theory demands that they should.

Perhaps one of the most important clashes of ideas, in theory and practice, is about how governments should use and understand the term "growth." Should they continue to track gross domestic product (GDP) and its propensity to grow, aware of the way it distorts success by averaging out the wealth of the poorest and the richest, encouraging a simplistic bottom line? Or should they be more suspicious because growth as conventionally measured may be ramming up against the limits of the planet's carrying capacity? In practice, "inclusive growth" has come to stand for a position midway between the two—where both the need for increasing prosperity and social equality are taken into account in economic decisions. But linking growth and equality in decision-making begs the question about the kinds of economic tools that will be required, and how much both need to be limited by environmental needs and limits.

Other modern economists wrestle with Garrett Hardin's so-called "Tragedy of the Commons," the title of his 1968 essay, which means that, although the economic decisions by all the farmers on former common land may be rational in theory—they all maximize their grazing until the land is overwhelmed—it is not necessarily rational for the group as a whole. Hardin's paradox was not from an economist;

he was actually an ecologist. These are just some of the dilemmas for the new kind of economics that is emerging from its straitjacket of the last few decades. You will find them reflected in this book.

A two-handed approach

"Give me a one-handed economist!" wailed US president Woodrow Wilson. "They all just say 'on the one hand, on the other hand.'" This is a short book and, as a dictionary of economic debate, it has only 52 entries. You would need to have an almost infinite number of hands to cover everything. We are also guilty of Wilson's accusation: we have tried to be even-handed. Where there are other views, or key debates, we have tried to include them.

The world beyond economics tends to look to economists for a lead. Perhaps they do so rather less these days, after their very public failure when the banks failed. But economists also have an understanding of the way that statistics, money flows, and human beings behave in the face of motivation, which makes them excellent figures to have inside any organization that creates public policy—even if, in recent years there may have been sometimes just too many of them. The World Bank, in its great years of expansion under the former American Defense Secretary Robert McNamara, employed ten times more economists than sociologists. It may be that the World Bank failures would not have been quite so egregious in those years if they had leavened the economics loaf a little. It might have helped them see a little more clearly.

It is probably right that the economics profession frustrates politicians who want clear answers. It is a young discipline, having emerged only in the final decades of the eighteenth century—a product of the Enlightenment, as it broke from the moral theology that had dominated medieval economics. There remain unanswered questions and one-handed economists because that is as far as economics has developed.

The biggest questions are up for grabs as never before, and they emerge at a moment of unprecedented crisis—not just political, but also planetary, which is why we have devoted a whole chapter to the economics of the Earth. It is not the fault of economists if politicians occasionally forget what is most important.

Our intention with this book has been to make our small contribution to the future of economics so that the next wave of economic understanding might be that much more likely to be done with a two-handed, two-eyed clarity about the wider world and the way that people really behave. So that economics can set aside its period of single-eyed adolescence—and grow up to become the savior of mankind.

How to use this book

This book distills the current body of knowledge into 52 manageable chunks, allowing you to skim-read or delve in deeper. There are four chapters, each containing 13 topics, prefaced by a set of biographies of key economists and a timeline of significant milestones. An introduction to each chapter then gives an overview of some of the key concepts you might need to navigate.

“People of the same trade seldom meet together, even for merriment and diversion, but the conversation ends in a conspiracy against the public, or in some contrivance to raise prices.”

ADAM SMITH,
THE WEALTH OF NATIONS (1776)

1 ECONOMIC HISTORY

INTRODUCTION

There are many aspects of medieval life that it is next to impossible to feel nostalgic about: heresy trials, dental practices, droit de seigneur, and so on. And yet the evidence points to a society that enjoyed longer vacation periods than we do, and had the means to construct cathedrals that would be beyond our means today. We may wonder why—despite two centuries of economic growth—we cannot afford lives or cathedrals anything like those. The fact is, we tend not to study economic history in the traditional way, regarding everything that went before as the necessary precursor to what we have today.

And yet this approach—looking at the history of ideas around money and wealth as arising out of the spirit and condition of the times—is coming back into fashion. That is the subject of this chapter. The march of time has not been inevitable. Economic history looks at those ways not traveled, and as a result, has not been altogether welcome in recent years in the ivory towers of academic economics. That is as good a reason as any for looking at it more closely now.

The road to modern economics

We start with issues at the heart of stone age economics and the origins of money (pages 20–21)—still the subject of a fiery debate among economic anthropologists—before moving on to medieval economics (pages 22–23). Modern economics emerged out of the moral philosophy of Adam Smith; it is hardly surprising, then, that medieval economics was based on theology and questions about what is right and wrong in our economic relations with each other. Credit and debt are the subject that follow (pages 24–25), being the issue that divides the medieval world from the modern one. In fact, you could say that modern economics began when debt became acceptable.

Next comes an entry on mercantilism (pages 26–27)—the doctrine that dominated the age of exploration, when trade was a zero-sum game, where its manipulation lay at the heart of imperial policy. This was the idea in economics that gave way to the classical economic notion that trade lifts all boats. Classical economics (pages 28–29), in turn, lies at the core of economic beliefs in all ages—and survives still, despite criticism.

The founding of the Bank of England in 1694, originally an innovative method of financing war with France, ushered in a period when central banks (pages 30–31) began to regulate an otherwise largely unregulated—or at least self-regulated—financial system. Only 60 years earlier, Europe had experienced the peculiar phenomenon of mass economic panic, with "tulipmania" in Holland. Soaring, but short-lived, prices for certain tulip varieties led to the scenario of thrill followed by collapse that still characterizes the bubbles and crashes we experience today (pages 34–35).

Unemployment (pages 32–33)—experienced on a huge scale after the Napoleonic Wars in the early nineteenth century—was another type of economic failure to make waves on a political level, especially in the early years of mass democracy.

Developments in the twentieth century

The two entries that follow set out the stalls of the two major camps in economic theory over the past 80 years or so. Both emerging out of the economic turmoil of the 1930s, the pioneers of Keynesian economics (pages 36–37) and the Chicago School and the Austrians (pages 38–39) approached matters from different, though related, viewpoints. Their arguments continue to echo through the political economy.

Globalization (pages 40–41) and austerity (pages 42–43) are both economic buzzwords without which it would be largely impossible to understand the recent economic debate—which is why we have included them in this first chapter. And many people would regard the advent of the "quants"—the number crunchers and mathematical physicists who took up residence in the financial capitals from the end of the twentieth century—as historically vital, because it explains some of the automation and historical blindness that led to the global financial crisis of 2007–8.

Indeed, all of the ideas in this chapter are vital for understanding the history and development of economic ideas through the ages. There is inevitably some overlap between this chapter and the one that follows, but our objective with this book has been to set out as much of the evidence as we can and then let you—the reader—make up your mind. Over to you!

TIMELINE

314

A BAN ON USURY

The modern global economy is based on debt—the creating and lending of money charged out at interest. But for much of history, simply earning money from money is generally condemned. It is outlawed by the early Christian Church when the Council of Arles bans clerics from lending money at interest.

1349

BLACK DEATH

The Great Plague forges across Europe, bringing an abrupt end to the greatest centuries of the expansion of trade, during which time roads and bridges are built, and new techniques in navigation and book-keeping are developed to track profitability on the high seas.

1600

EAST INDIA COMPANY

"John Company," as it is known, becomes the first modern corporation, given a royal charter by Queen Elizabeth I to trade with the East. It becomes increasingly concerned with consolidating its power over India, with a private army of a quarter of a million—twice the size of the British Army at the time.

1637

TULIPMANIA

The bizarre phenomenon in the Netherlands whereby speculation in tulip bulbs leads to the best examples being exchanged for more than ten times the annual salary of a skilled craftsperson, or sometimes for the value of an entire mansion. This episode is the first example of a speculative bubble.

THE WEALTH OF NATIONS

Adam Smith's classic is published the same year as the American Declaration of Independence and owes something to the same bundle of Enlightenment ideas. The book is one of the founding documents of classical economics, introducing ideas like the hidden hand, the division of labor, and productivity.

1846

REPEAL OF THE CORN LAWS

The UK Corn Laws, put in place after the Napoleonic Wars, are designed to help domestic landowners by taxing imports, but result in increased living costs for others. Their repeal is the symbolic beginning of the era of free trade that dominates the Victorian period.

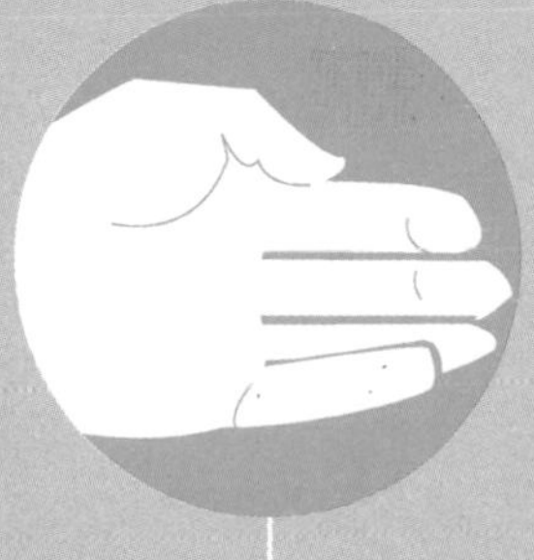

1929

WALL STREET CRASH

The collapse of the stock market in October 1929 marks the end of the so-called Roaring Twenties and the start of the Great Depression. A series of terrifying lurches wipes 83 percent off the value of American investments. With every lurch, the shares underwriting people's loans lose value, too.

2015

NEW CHALLENGES

When the world signs the Paris Agreement on climate change, it agrees "to limit the temperature increase to 1.5°C [34.7°F] above pre-industrial levels." This sets a global carbon budget for an economy still dependent on fossil fuels, which means rapid and radical change is unavoidable.

BIOGRAPHIES

DAVID RICARDO (1722–1823)

Born in England, the son of a stockbroker, David Ricardo eloped with a Quaker, changed his faith (which resulted in him being disowned by his father), and went on to become rich from speculating over the result of the Battle of Waterloo. He was part of an influential circle of thinkers including Jeremy Bentham (see page 52) and Thomas Robert Malthus, and together with Malthus, attended James Mill's Political Economy Club. Ricardo was socially liberal, an abolitionist, and also an ardent free trader. His theory that general benefits result from countries specializing in what they trade—"comparative advantage"—proved profoundly influential in the development of globalization. But often overlooked were the necessary conditions for it to work, such as finance not being mobile. Ricardo's famous example of free trade between England and Portugal, for example (see page 68), in practice resulted in Portugal's long-standing economic underdevelopment. Ricardo, like several prominent early economists, believed that economic development would tend toward a "stationary state" where further growth would not be necessary.

JOHN MAYNARD KEYNES (1883–1946)

"His radical idea that governments should spend money they don't have may have saved capitalism" said *Time* magazine in 1999, marking the beginning of a resurgence of influence by the great economist J. M. Keynes. Born in Cambridge, England, Keynes won a scholarship to King's College, where he read mathematics, before going on to join the civil service at the India Office in London. He quickly mastered the intricacies of Indian currency reform, and became a trusted adviser to Prime Minister David Lloyd George at the disastrous negotiations that led to the Treaty of Versailles in 1919. Convinced that the treaty would be economically disastrous for Europe as a whole, Keynes wrote his famous book *The Economic Consequences of the Peace*. He was deeply influenced by the failure of conventional economic ideas to deal with the Great Depression and came to believe that, left to itself, the economy may not simply recover, but would require injections of money to stimulate demand. Keynesian economics went out of fashion after the "stagflation" of the 1970s.

FRIEDRICH AUGUST VON HAYEK (1899–1992)

The economist and philosopher Friedrich Hayek was born in Austria, and in 1917 joined the army to fight on the Italian front. After the war he attended the University of Vienna, studying law, political science, philsophy, and economics. He was a key figure in the Vienna School of prewar, free-market economists, working for Ludwig von Mises, and becoming an expert in the way prices signal and coordinate people's buying. From 1932, at the London School of Economics, Hayek was involved in public debates with Keynes about where the government could invest most effectively. Hayek became a British citizen in 1938, just before World War II, and his most famous work was written there—*The Road to Serfdom*, a warning against economic planning and technocracy, published during a paper shortage in 1944. It was this book that gave a political impetus to the so-called Austrian School of economic thought, which met in 1947 in Mont Pèlerin and has since gone on to dominate economics. Like Keynes, Hayek studied the business cycle, but Hayek suggested that it fluctuates because of periods when money is too easy to borrow.

ANNA SCHWARTZ (1915–2012)

Anna Schwartz was born in New York City, studied economics at Columbia University, then went on to work at the National Bureau of Economic Research, where she remained for the rest of her career. Despite being one of the leading monetary scholars of all time, Schwartz was the lesser-known coauthor of what is probably the most influential book on monetary economics written since World War II. In 1963, she and the future Nobel Prize–winning economist Milton Friedman published *A Monetary History of the United States, 1867–1960*. Among other things, the book blamed the Federal Reserve for causing the Great Depression. Schwartz did not share the Nobel Prize with Friedman (the awarding committee stated that the book was "one of Friedman's most profound and also most distinguished achievements"). Partly as a result of this book, which came out of the famous Chicago School of economic thought (see page 38), governments around the world began to focus on monetary policy to manage their economies.

WHERE DID IT ALL START?

THE MAIN CONCEPT | *Stone Age Economics* was the title of an influential collection of essays published in 1972 by the American anthropologist Marshall Sahlins, which set out the battle lines around an issue that economics had never really grappled with before—where did money come from and why? The academic argument rages between the so-called formalists and the substantivists, and Sahlins led the substantivists into battle—with the idea that culture came before economic necessity. But the real argument is between those who think that money emerged because of trade between tribes, and those who think it emerged in the culture of gifts between families. Anthropologists believe that evidence seems to point toward their view, that economic relations took shape as a way of giving things to mark treaties, or rituals, or marriages, and only then began to develop a more formal whiff of economics. For example, the visit to Solomon by the Queen of Sheba around 950 BCE, armed with spices, gold, and precious stones, seems to have been about overwhelming the other side with demonstrations of generosity. And the word "pay" comes from the Latin *pacare*, which means to pacify, appease, or make peace with. Money began as a way to make peace. In other words, economic relationships emerged from giving and peacemaking, and not the other way around.

DRILL DOWN | Another view emerges from the study of the very first coins, supposedly among the Lydians in what is now Turkey, in around the seventh century BCE. According to the historian Herodotus, the Lydians were also the first recorded pimps, so would have used the coins as a way of being extremely precise about price and debt in a way they never could before. Behind the formalist/substantivist argument lie different attitudes to the nature of humanity—are we basically generous or avaricious? If the Lydians really invented coins to facilitate prostitution, then the answer may be more complex: we started generous but soon wanted something in return.

FOCUS | *"The worst thing is not giving presents. We give what we have. That is the way we live together." That is how a Kalahari bushman expressed the origins of economics, as quoted in the writer William Bloom's book* Money, Heart and Mind *(1995).*

MEDIEVAL ECONOMICS
Page 22
UTILITY & RATIONAL ECONOMIC MAN
Page 56
THE CORE ECONOMY
Page 110

MEDIEVAL ECONOMICS

THE MAIN CONCEPT | It is a strange idea, but there was a time when economics, and economic policy, were highly influenced by the Church. Considerations of profit and loss were considered subservient to the concept of the just price—although market forces were clearly important (otherwise nobody would buy and sell) there was also an underlying justice that needed to come first. Anyone who lent so much that the recipient could not pay it back, or charged too much—taking advantage of the desperation of their clients—were accused of being usurers. In fact, until the Reformation, the Church frowned on anyone who charged interest, which meant that most lending had to be done by official outsiders, mainly the Jewish community. The idea that there was an appropriate moral price to charge could only work in an age that was still ignorant of the "quantity theory of money" (that prices are directly related to the amount of money in circulation), although the basic morality behind it is shared by most people to this day: inflation aside, they don't like to be ripped off, even in the name of "market forces."

PRICE
Page 66

THE SHARING ECONOMY
Page 112

THE CIRCULAR ECONOMY
Page 130

DRILL DOWN | It takes courage sometimes to step out of the thinking that files everything medieval in a locked cabinet marked "brutality," "ignorance," or "superstition"—aspects of medieval economics need a second look. When archaeologists unearth skeletons in London from the twelfth century, they are as tall, and therefore as well fed, as skeletons in any other period of history except our own. Their society also built some of the great structures of the world. We may not want to go back there, but it is worth wondering why—despite two centuries of economic growth—we are unable to afford cathedrals anything like theirs. Working conditions also compare unfavorably. Victorian economists calculated that the average English peasant in 1485 needed to work 15 weeks a year to earn enough for a year. In 1564, it was 40 weeks, and it has only got worse.

FOCUS | *It is easy to dismiss medieval economics, but it did not hold back the massive expansion of European trade. However, the Black Death in the 1340s brought total collapse—and the weight of goods traded failed to recover to the same position until the seventeenth century.*

CREDIT & DEBT

THE MAIN CONCEPT | Credit means you borrow money—sometimes from the bank, sometimes from some other unregulated business or loan shark, or sometimes just by delaying paying an invoice. And when someone extends credit to you, they create a debt, as well as the money to eventually pay it off (but not the extra interest they charge, of course). This is known as "credit creation," and the task of central banks is to ensure there is enough credit being created to keep the economy going, yet not so much new money sloshing around that it leads to higher prices—too much money chasing too few goods means inflation. Debt may also be necessary for a functioning economy (it allows companies and individuals to invest in order to earn money later), but a great weight of debt—piled on by less-regulated institutions like hedge funds—can also be enormously damaging, as it was in the run-up to the financial crisis of 2007–8. From the 1990s onward, economists and other commentators began to warn about the dangers of too much debt—for nations and individuals. Debts hang heavily on those who experience the world of money as a concrete, inflexible, punitive thing. But if you are already wealthy, you can expect the world of credit to be forgiving and fluid and to lend almost whatever you need to make dreams come true—as long as they believe you will pay it back.

DRILL DOWN | It now seems pretty clear, though the idea is still controversial, that most of the money in circulation is created in the form of debt by banks or mortgage providers. Notes and coins are put into circulation without interest attached, but they only make up about 3 percent of the money we use. This gives banks a huge unearned income, known as "seigniorage," in return for the risk of lending the money into existence. It also explains why debt hangs heavily over the economy, because the interest to pay it back has not been created at the same time. The theory is that investments will grow and we will be able to afford it.

FOCUS | *One of the ironies of credit and debt is that, although available to most of us in the developed world, the richest pay considerably less than the poorest, who are forced to visit loan sharks, charging up to 5,000 percent APR—and who are frequently reported to threaten to break your legs, or your family's legs, if you fail to keep up your scheduled repayments.*

CENTRAL BANKS
Page 30

GREAT BUBBLES & CRASHES
Page 34

INFLATION
Page 64

MERCANTILISM

THE MAIN CONCEPT | Mercantilism was the name given to the imperial trade policy that dominated much of Europe from the sixteenth to the eighteenth century. It was an aggressive, expansionist idea—unlike protectionism, which is simply defensive—based on maximizing exports and minimizing imports, at the same time. This usually meant establishing high tariff barriers to prevent people buying imported goods; and if other nations tried to do the same, then you simply sent a gunboat—or, in really difficult cases, your whole fleet—to force the other side to trade with you, on beneficial terms. At its heart was the idea that the most important thing, and the basis of a nation's wealth, was its reserves of gold and silver bullion. People like Sir Josiah Child, a financier and East India Company pioneer—a man who was capable of bribing monarchs—developed these ideas at the end of the seventeenth century. And however much mercantilism is dismissed by economists in modern debate, the idea still remains potent to this day. You can see it operating in Chinese trade policy, while the old mercantile ideas are on the rise again in the economics of, for example, Donald Trump. The problem with mercantilism is that only one side can win—not everyone, by definition, can have a positive trade balance. The question is: does it really matter if they don't?

DRILL DOWN | It was the classical economist Adam Smith who torpedoed mercantilism with the growing realization that the inevitable result of mercantilism was war—or at least high spending on weapons, navies, and armies. That meant high taxes. It also meant economic oppression for the working classes. It was far more efficient, said Smith and those who followed him, if trade barriers were kept low and people could trade freely with each other and buy what they could not provide for themselves from specialists. Result: peace, harmony, and wealth—or so they said. Mercantilism implies monopoly power, while free trade implies small businesses competing with each other, but not fighting. In reality, the era of supposed free trade has also seen the rise of enormous monopoly power via large global corporations.

CLASSICAL ECONOMICS
Page 28
THE INVISIBLE HAND
Page 54
COMPARATIVE ADVANTAGE
Page 68

FOCUS | *When the English seized the port of New Amsterdam in 1664—now New York City—it was a mercantilist dream that drove them on: to take by force the key trading points in the world and to make sure the locals produced raw materials for the home market and would trade with nobody but the British. It was one of the factors that led to chafing against foreign rule in any empire, and especially among the Americans—hence the American War of Independence.*

CLASSICAL ECONOMICS

THE MAIN CONCEPT | Classical economics was a school of thought that developed in the eighteenth century; it showed that prosperity need not require conflict, and that trade might not be a zero-sum game after all. As the doctrine that took over from the old mercantilist ideas, its principles formed the foundations of modern economic thought. Adam Smith's book *An Inquiry into the Nature and Causes of the Wealth of Nations* (1776) was published in the same year as the American Revolution, and was itself a reaction against the Jacobite uprising under Bonnie Prince Charlie. Smith and fellow classical economist David Ricardo demonstrated that everyone pursuing their own best interests might produce prosperity for everyone, via what Smith called the "invisible hand" of the market—the sum of billions of small decisions. The other central idea at the heart of this whole bundle of beliefs was much more debatable: that any economy is always either moving toward equilibrium or has actually reached it. This was so in the labor market and capital market, just as interest rates made sure there was always a balance between savings and investment in the economy. Critics of classical economics might accept that the invisible hand works, in a sense, but they dismiss the belief in equilibrium as a theological doctrine backed by no obvious evidence.

DRILL DOWN | One of the fiercest and most effective critics of classical economics was J. M. Keynes (see also page 36), whose 1936 *General Theory of Employment, Interest and Money* turned conventional economic doctrine on its head. If economies tend toward equilibrium, he wondered, then why did the Great Depression get increasingly deeper? He saw that it was a speculative bond market that actually decided interest rates, rather than any kind of equilibrium. He also understood that it was far harder, in practice, to cut people's wages than to raise them; when demand falls in an economy, it may not make workers cheaper and prices lower—it will probably just create unemployment.

FOCUS | *The problem with classical economics is that it is a set of beliefs—or at least "models" of the economy—that often bear little relation to the real world. Equilibrium might indeed be possible if everyone had the same resources and economic clout, but they don't in the real world, where wealthy people can profit from downturns as much as they will from economic booms.*

KEYNSIAN ECONOMICS
Page 36
THE INVISIBLE HAND
Page 54
COMPARATIVE ADVANTAGE
Page 68

CENTRAL BANKS

THE MAIN CONCEPT | The very first central bank—the Riksbank, later renamed Sveriges Riksbank—was set up in Sweden in 1668. This was then copied in 1694 by the English, who set up the Bank of England (originally as a way of paying for a war with France), which itself went on to provide the model for most central banks today. These days, central banks have three main tasks before them—setting short-term interest rates, making sure the institutions of the economy are healthy (including assessing how sound the banking system is), and being a so-called lender of last resort—lending to struggling banks when nobody else will. They also tend to manage currency transactions and borrowing for the government of the day, selling Treasury bonds, or Treasury bills (T-bonds or T-bills). There has been a recent trend of making central banks independent, though of course this is also a polite fiction—and they often have an inflation rate target they must meet—in order to give them the space to decide on the best long-term interests of the economy. There has also been some criticism of the way that some central banks have pursued a "quantitative easing" policy (injecting new money into the economy), which was bound to make rich people wealthier, yet leave others untouched.

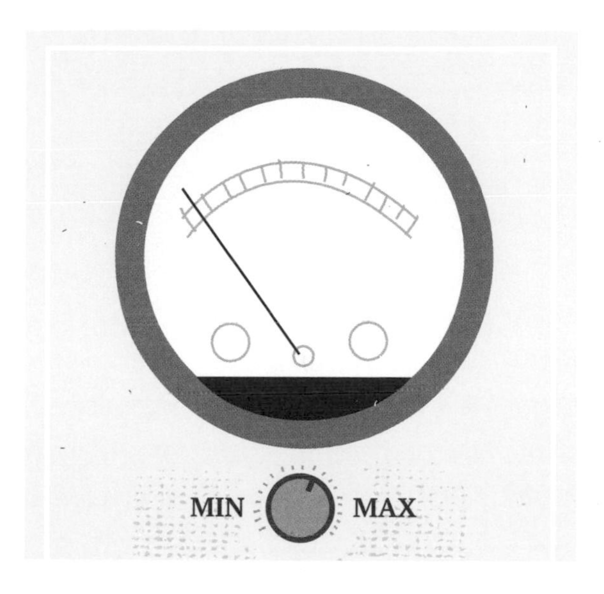

DRILL DOWN | Unlike in most countries, the whole idea of a central bank was deeply controversial in the US, where many prior to independence had resisted the notion of coming under the control of the Bank of England. They only got round to launching one (the Federal Reserve) in 1913, on their third attempt—President Andrew Jackson refused to renew the charter of the second one and it went bust in 1841. Even then the Fed's influence is dispersed widely across the country, with different roles for each office. The Federal Reserve of New York looks after the gold reserves of many nations (though not the US, which keeps its gold at Fort Knox in Kentucky). Americans traditionally distrust banks and bankers, fearing that a central bank will push out democratic limits to banking power.

FOCUS | *Montagu Norman was Governor of the Bank of England from 1920 to 1944. He was a patient of the psychologist Carl Jung, who famously said that Norman was mad. One story suggests that he crossed the Atlantic in disguise as a "Professor Skinner" in 1929, for a secret meeting with American monetary officials and to introduce a short monetary shock to force the US back on the gold standard. Instead, the shock resulted in the Great Depression. Or so the story goes.*

GREAT BUBBLES & CRASHES
Page 34

KEYNESIAN ECONOMICS
Page 36

MACROECONOMICS & MICROECONOMICS
Page 60

UNEMPLOYMENT

THE MAIN CONCEPT | Unemployment is one of the tragedies of economies. People lack the money to pay for food and shelter, and then slowly drop out of the social networks that can get them back into paid work. It is also one of the great mysteries of economics—if economies tend toward some kind of equilibrium, as the classical economists say, then it is not clear why the business cycle (see page 72) should be so dominant in almost every economy, and joblessness rises and falls with this cycle. Unemployment isn't as simple as a percentage figure of the population, either, which is how it is usually expressed. In that same figure is "structural unemployment," which is the joblessness that is immune to any upturn. There is also "voluntary unemployment," where people have deliberately downshifted to earn less—sometimes much less—or to change their lives in other ways. There are those people who, for health or mental health reasons, find it impossible to hold down a job. There are also those who are just between jobs for whatever reason, who may make up the basic underlying unemployment rate of 1 or 2 percent. Whether you believe unemployment is a scourge that economists need to tackle above all else, or whether you think that, like the poor, they are always with us, depends on what kind of economist you are.

DRILL DOWN | What you think about the reasons for unemployment will tend to determine your favored solution. If you think it is primarily the result of a downturn in the business cycle, then you may want to increase demand in the economy. There is a proven link between lower unemployment and rising inflation, a relationship expressed as the Phillips curve. If, on the other hand, you think that inflation is a more fundamental evil, and are frustrated that wages don't fall during business downturns, then you might favor deregulating the labor market rules to make labor more flexible, in an attempt to fix the supply and demand for labor into some kind of balance.

FOCUS | *Some people predict that we may all soon be out of a job, thanks to the rise of robots and artificial intelligence. There have been suggestions that we must therefore break the link between employment and income. That would mean the state paying every citizen a basic income as a right—produced out of taxation or some kind of quantitative easing—and letting the money trickle up through the economy rather than trickling down.*

KEYNESIAN ECONOMICS
Page 36
PRODUCTIVITY
Page 58
DEMAND & SUPPLY
Page 62

GREAT BUBBLES & CRASHES

THE MAIN CONCEPT | Because the urge to get rich quickly and cheaply is easy to exploit, speculative bonanzas can be sporadically whipped up into such intensity that it can bring down a whole financial system. "Tulipmania" in the Netherlands in the 1630s was one of the first bubbles of the modern world. Tulip jobbers speculated in the rise and fall in the price of tulip bulbs, and many grew rich overnight when bulbs began to reach extraordinary prices, the rarest being sold for great fortunes. Strange stories circulated about people who bought them thinking they were onions, ate them by mistake, then found they had consumed the value of a large mansion. Then the bottom dropped out of the market; the speculators were ruined and aristocrats were forced to mortgage their estates. Everyone vowed it would never happen again. But it always does, and following the same patterns: a belief that some new technological or economic breakthrough has permanently changed the way markets react; doubters are publicly ridiculed, funds for useful projects dry up, and there are assurances that this time it will be different. And so on, right through to the global financial crisis of 2007–8. It is the way of the economic world.

KEYNESIAN ECONOMICS
Page 36
THE RISE OF THE QUANTS
Page 44
ECONOMIC CYCLES
Page 72

DRILL DOWN | In 1716, the Scottish financier John Law persuaded the French government to set up what would later become the Banque Royale, through which he issued large numbers of bank notes that were to be underpinned by profits from his speculative Mississippi Company. There were riots at the Bourse in Paris as people fought, and even sold their bodies, for the right to buy shares. The Banque Royale was soon so successful that Law agreed to take on the entire French national debt; he turned it into paper and became the richest man in the world. It is said that the resulting crash was so desperate that it may have caused the French Revolution nearly three-quarters of a century later.

FOCUS | *Keynes warned against bubbles in his 1936* General Theory of Employment, Interest and Money: *"Speculators may do no harm as bubbles on a steady stream of enterprise, but the position is serious when enterprise becomes the bubble on a whirlpool of speculation."*

KEYNESIAN ECONOMICS

THE MAIN CONCEPT | The Great Depression lasted for most of the 1930s, and is said to have begun with the shock of the Wall Street Crash in October 1929, when the values of people's investments collapsed on the American markets. What followed led to up to one third of the workforce on both sides of the Atlantic finding themselves out of work, and about half the banks in the US—which had been the cheerleaders of the Roaring Twenties—shutting their doors. That desperate situation seems to have been made worse by the policies brought in to respond to it, including high tariff barriers and controls on lending money. The Depression also provided the backdrop to a major rethink of economic policies, developed primarily by the English economist J. M. Keynes, which were designed to borrow money in order to increase demand. Economics was about life, Keynes stated, and without money, people would die. The most immediate and famous manifestation of Keynesian-style economics came with the New Deal, under the presidency of Franklin Roosevelt, who characterized the economic problem as having "nothing to fear but fear itself." The New Deal provided employment for artists, writers, road-builders, and dam-builders, alongside a whole variety of other projects designed to help people out of poverty and back to work.

CLASSICAL ECONOMICS
Page 28
AUSTERITY
Page 42
INFLATION
Page 64

DRILL DOWN | Keynesian economics in practice reached acceptance after his death in 1946. They were only loosely based on the ideas of the great man, but they came to dominate policy after World War II as world leaders attempted to get rid of the business cycle altogether by borrowing and investing more in the lean years, and paying it back out of the so-called "multiplier" effect, which meant that the same money circulated over and over again, and every time it recirculated, it could be taxed. Was Keynesianism to blame for the inflation of the 1970s? Or was that the abuse of Keynesian principles to pay for the Vietnam War? "We are all Keynesian now," said US president Richard Nixon, and that is how he spent the money.

FOCUS | *Keynes was not a technocrat. His ideas had a moral edge, and were a critique of economics without a human purpose. "We are capable of shutting off the sun and the stars because they do not pay a dividend," he wrote in 1933. In other words, we need to be able to see beyond monetary values.*

THE CHICAGO SCHOOL

THE MAIN CONCEPT | The so-called Chicago School of economics, with its emphasis on deregulation, low inflation, and monetarism, emerged from the economics department at Chicago University in the 1930s under Henry Simon—at the time, a hotbed for radical thinking. But it was a book by another liberal, Friedrich von Hayek, that started the ball rolling. *The Road to Serfdom* (1944) was approved by J. M. Keynes and it has never been out of print. Hayek and his fellow Austrians were anti-Nazis, keen on the idea of free markets as an antidote to state technocracy. They met to promote their ideas at Mont Pèlerin in Switzerland in 1947. The question of who should write an American version of *The Road* then sparked infighting at the new Chicago School, and the third person to try was the monetarist Milton Friedman. His version, *Capitalism and Freedom*, was published in 1962. Friedman changed Hayek's approach in some critical ways—notably his skepticism about monopoly being a problem. The Austrian School and the Chicago School—one a linked group of thinkers, the other a bricks-and-mortar institution—remained in the wilderness until the doldrums of the 1970s, and the subsequent arrival of Margaret Thatcher and Ronald Reagan, who put their ideas into practice.

GLOBALIZATION
Page 40

THE INVISIBLE HAND
Page 54

MONOPOLIES
Page 74

DRILL DOWN | Hayek was influenced by another economist from the University of Vienna, Ludwig von Mises, after which, he said, "the world was never the same again." Hayek became known for his theory of business cycles, which he said were caused by mistaken investments paid for by money created by banks. But it was only after the death of Keynes that Hayek joined the Chicago School and became known for his revolt against the technocratic idea that institutions or policy-makers know better than people what is good for them. Through Hayek, the Austrians and the Chicago School became, in effect, one tradition. He lived to see the adoption of many of his ideas before he died.

FOCUS | *This is how Hayek put it: "I do not think it is an exaggeration to say history is largely a history of inflation, usually inflations engineered by governments for the gain of governments."*

GLOBALIZATION

THE MAIN CONCEPT | The Americans have come to define the bundle of ideas around globalization, but the original word was coined by the French: *mondialisation*. However, if the original idea simply meant that products and services were becoming increasingly global, from the 1970s onward, the term became increasingly contested and specific—especially with the growth of multinational businesses and speculation in money values after 1979 (the year that the UK decided to end exchange controls on money leaving the country). Some felt that the trade deals and subsidies given to multinational corporations gave them unnecessary advantages, arguing that globalization constituted governments divesting themselves of their own powers and responsibilities and selling them off to the multinationals. The other driver of globalization has been the peculiar world of financialization—again, driven initially by the decision made by the UK in 1979, which has meant that organizations have increasingly tried to outsource all their functions bar the financial ones. By the turn of the century, financial flows across the world were more than $4 trillion a day, most of it speculation. A critical consensus is emerging that judges globalization to mean that the ultra-wealthy make money in downturns as well as upturns, using sophisticated financial algorithms—termed "plutonomy" by Citigroup.

THE CHICAGO SCHOOL
Page 38
THE RISE OF THE QUANTS
Page 44
MONOPOLIES
Page 74

DRILL DOWN | Although globalization is considered a modern phenomenon, there have been other periods of huge global financial flows—for example, before 1914; in fact the flow of trade did not recover to its pre-World War I levels until 1990. And medieval trade before the Black Death was hardly marked by financial flows, but it did mark a European high point in multinational trade links. What, then, is distinct about our own era of globalization? Critics claim that it is the suppression of local variety by ubiquitous global products. Supporters claim that globalization has improved billions of lives. Critics reply that, while that is so, it has also led to serious gulfs between rich and poor.

FOCUS | *What is the symbol of globalization? Some writers have claimed it was the Lexus car in the 1990s. Or the Big Mac, which was used by the* Economist *magazine as the basis for cost comparisons between nations. Later, it was the Samsung or Motorola cell phone. Now it may be the dominance of vitual brands like Amazon, Google, and Facebook.*

AUSTERITY

THE MAIN CONCEPT | "Austerity" is a troublesome word. It sounds unpleasant, like "puritanism." It describes a kind of hair-shirted determination to reduce public spending. It was the way that the postwar UK Labour government, elected in 1945, described their policy to pay back unrepayable war loans, taken out to survive World War II—though they still managed to launch a version of the welfare state and to kickstart a national health service. The word was revived in economics after the 2007–8 banking crash, when a number of countries publicly committed themselves to austerity policies, mainly to restore the confidence of the financial markets in their ability to pay their debts. This was also the policy that was forced on struggling nations like Greece to prevent them from defaulting on debts, and which arguably reduced many Greeks to poverty. Controversy still surrounds the idea of austerity because the big banks remain powerful, and those who run them still earn bankers' salaries—when they were responsible for the financial disaster. Ordinary people lose out but banks are considered critical to any kind of recovery, so they are protected.

DRILL DOWN | The alternative to austerity after financial crises is to reflate the economy by borrowing, and to apply the palette of Keynesian policies (see page 36). This argument still rages. The UK government failed to pay off its debts using austerity policies, as Keynes might have predicted. But then the US government—which shunned austerity—did not manage to make much more of a success of their recovery than the UK did. Even so, only the most ardent advocates of austerity could believe that there is no limit to the idea, because it will in the end shrink the economy and tend toward bankruptcy. But what really undermines austerity is the politics of it—when it means that ordinary people must remain austere, while bankers are allowed to remain as profligate as ever.

DEMAND & SUPPLY
Page 62
MONETARISM
Page 70
ECONOMIC CYCLES
Page 72

FOCUS | *Austerity should not be dismissed entirely. It is a means by which the dead wood of the system is thrown out, organizations can renew themselves, innovation gets a kickstart, and ideas become important again. The difficulty, though, is that these may only be ideas about saving money, which may not be what is needed most.*

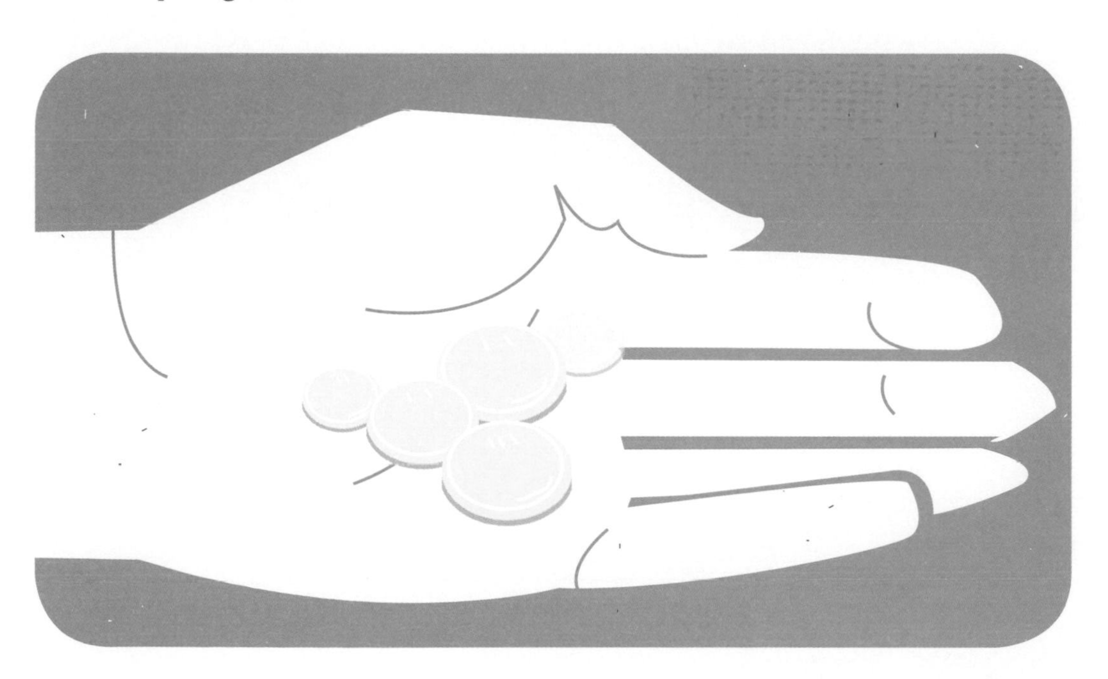

THE RISE OF THE QUANTS

THE MAIN CONCEPT | Quantitative finance uses a mathematical approach to analyze financial markets. The first true quantitative analyst, or "quant," was Harry Markowitz, whose 1954 doctoral thesis introduced the idea of applying high math and physics to finance. But it took another four decades before financial capitals around the world began to hire theoretical physicists and other mathematicians, partly because of the growth of hedge funds and automatic trading systems, as well as the increasing complexity of securities. How were accountants and traders supposed to price risk effectively, and to develop new products that did so, by looking at the underlying rate of the rate of the rate, for example of growth, which is where the term "derivatives" emerged? The answer: send for the quants. Their main task was to develop market-neutral investment systems that would mean that investments could be relied upon to go up in value, come what may. In fact, it was partly these kinds of products, which looked safe no matter what—because they mixed unsafe mortgage debts in with safe debts in the notorious "collateralized debt obligations" (CDOs)—that led to the financial crisis of 2007–8. Quants tend to specialize in a particular class of products, and because they are regarded as being the source of answers, they can command salaries of up to $500,000.

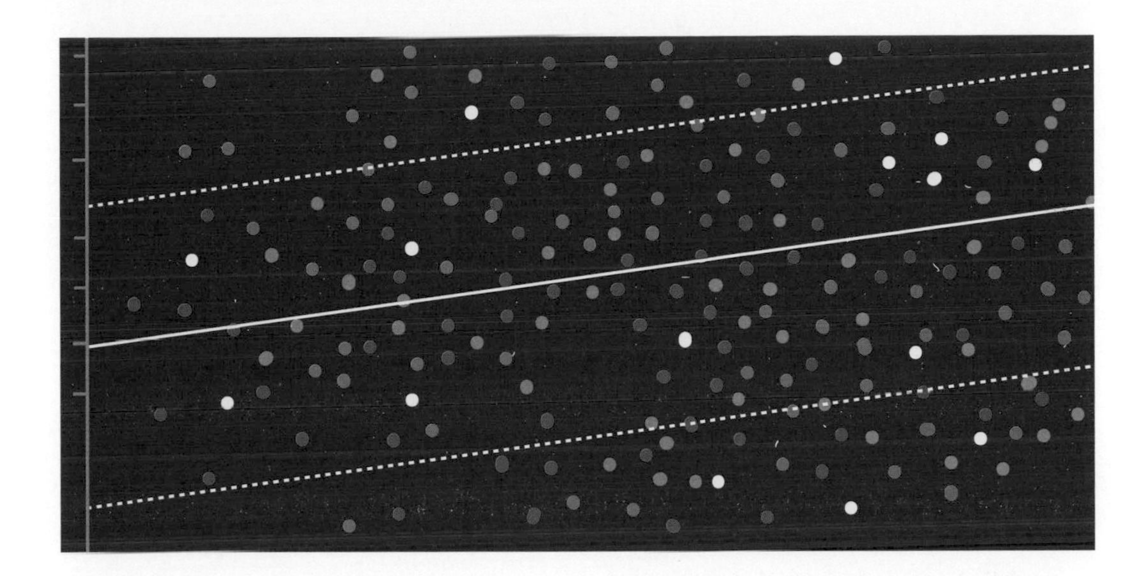

DRILL DOWN | The trouble with abstract models of the economy is that people don't always behave in the way that graphs or models say that they should. Economists don't claim that they do, but the increasing abstraction of the economics field has turned it from an art into a pseudoscience. In 1999, a revolt by economic graduate students at the Sorbonne in Paris claimed that abstract economics without history or human depth was ruining the discipline and removing it from reality. They demanded what they called a "post-autistic economics" (see page 82) instead.

FOCUS | *Is economics an art or a science? It certainly moves forward according to the evidence, as a science does, leaning on new paradigms that explain the world—until these break down and have to be replaced. However, the scientific models that economists use have to build in more variety than they can comfortably manage because of the peculiar ways in which people actually tend to behave—making them not very scientific.*

GREAT BUBBLES & CRASHES
Page 34

GLOBALIZATION
Page 40

MONETARISM
Page 70

“For at least another hundred years we must pretend to ourselves and to everyone that fair is foul and foul is fair; for foul is useful and fair is not. Avarice and usury and precaution must be our gods for a little longer still.”

JOHN MAYNARD KEYNES,
“ECONOMIC POSSIBILITIES FOR OUR GRANDCHILDREN” (1930)

BIG IDEAS

INTRODUCTION

Economics not only has opinions on everything, it has a full range of opinions on everything. There has traditionally been a diversity of views within one big picture, in which markets, private property, speculative finance, individualism, growth, and consumerism rule. Since the crisis of 2007–8, however, confidence in that model has been shaken. At the same time, interest has risen in a range of different perspectives that come from the study of complexity, neuro- and behavioral science, ecology, feminism, and the core economy of family, mutualism, and community.

Big ideas and big questions

These developments are a reminder that behind the ebb and flow of schools of thought that achieve temporary dominance, there is a constant battle of big ideas. Who has the right to make decisions over how the economy is run and how benefits should be distributed? About how much is enough and how much is too much, and the responsibilities we have for the people we may never meet, but who provide our food, clothes, and electronic devices? When you take away the novelty and distractions, economics is really an inquiry into how we should live in the world.

We begin this chapter with a discussion of the "invisible hand" (pages 54–55)—a concept introduced by Adam Smith that underpins much of classical economic thinking. Did Smith believe that this unseen force would create some kind of equilibrium? Or is this metaphysical hand something a little bit more useful, flexible, and humane? Then there is the concept of the rational economic man (pages 56–57). Is there any such person? Do we really maximize our happiness in the way the original economists thought?

We also look at the concept of productivity (pages 58–59)—a slippery idea that goes to the heart of the modern agonies about rising wealth and well-being. What kind of environmental, ethical, or cultural limits are there to rising productivity?

When we look at the great distinctions of economics, like macroeconomics versus microeconomics (pages 60–61) or demand versus supply (pages 62–63), each one of these tends to subtly change in meaning with every generation that goes by. A further distinction that we cover is inflation versus deflation (pages 64–65), together with the changes in how this is measured.

Price is another key issue (pages 66–67). We have to rely on price to allocate resources effectively in a modern economy, but there are clearly elements—important elements—that are in effect ignored by price. For example, what about human environmental costs?

The topic that follows is comparative advantage (pages 68–69), which, linked to free trade, now once again dominates so much debate about world trade, development, and regeneration. There are questions about the degree to which comparative advantage underpins the poverty of places that are already poor. In the same way, there are issues about free trade and how its meaning may have changed since the days of David Ricardo in the early nineteenth century.

Continuing debates

Nobody who wants to understand the debate about economics over the past generation can ignore monetarism (pages 70–71). The influential economist Milton Friedman and his ideas have dominated economics since they emerged in the 1960s, concerning the extent to which you can control inflation by having central banks squeeze the money supply—though at great cost to the economy.

There is also something slightly metaphysical about the debate around economic cycles (pages 72–73)—whether these are best explained as Kondratiev waves, lasting for more than 70 years, or whether cycles are much shorter than this. Gordon Brown's period in office as Chancellor of the Exchequer in the UK was dominated by his attempt to end the business cycle—which did not end well.

Two other issues dominating economic debate today are the growth and development of monopolies (pages 74–75) and complexity (pages 76–77). Complexity derives from ideas in scientific thinking in recent decades, especially around theoretical physics, which have made their mark on understanding the way financial world markets work. Which brings us to questions around efficient markets and market failure (pages 78–79), both of which mark opposite ends of the theoretical spectrum. It may be that economists failed to see the 2007–8 crash coming because efficient market theory suggested no such crash was possible, and there the debate rests. Once again, you must decide.

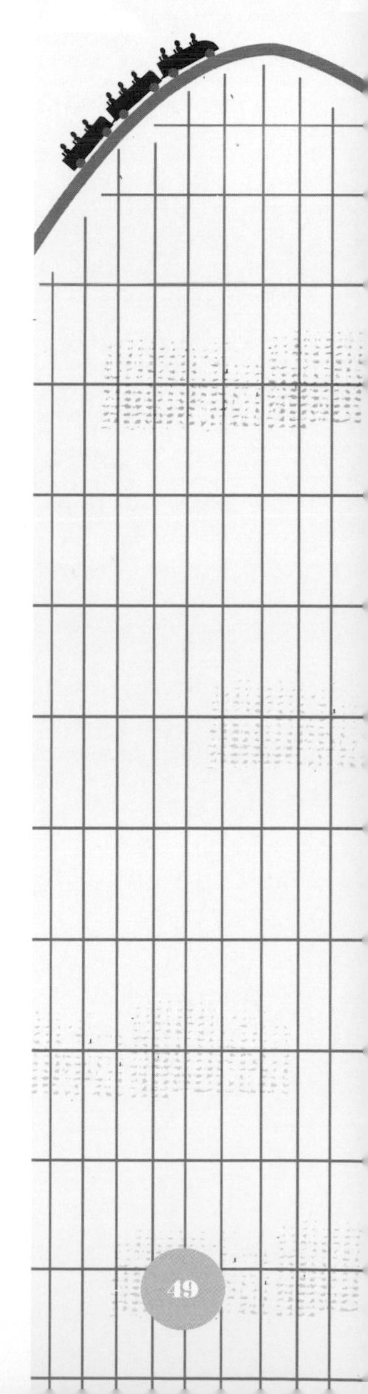

TIMELINE

ENCLOSURE

Beginning in England, and later spreading internationally, the process of enclosure allows barons and manorial lords to take common land for their own use, thereby altering the balance between private and public ownership, and concentrating power and wealth into fewer hands.

1668

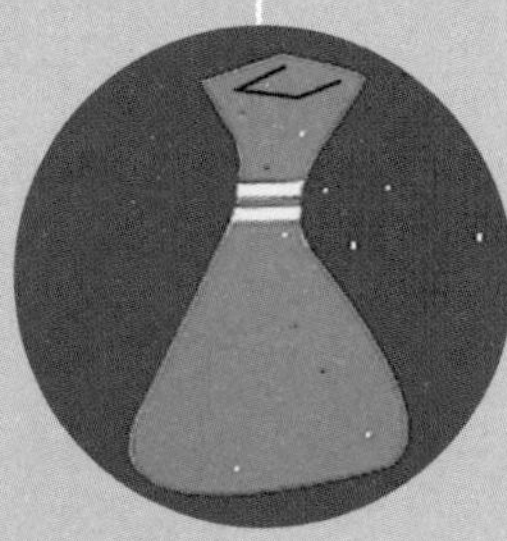

CENTRAL BANKS

The Swedish Riksbank—the world's first central bank—is founded, and assumes the power (later copied internationally) to control the bank's ratio of assets and lending. With "fractional-reserve banking," reserves held by banks need only be a small fraction of what they lend, giving them power to create money.

1844

COOPERATIVES

The modern cooperative movement begins with the Equitable Pioneers society in Rochdale, England. Cooperatives allow economic self-organization by communities faced with exploitatively priced, poor-quality goods. They share profits among members and remain a popular alternative to shareholder companies.

1862

LIMITED LIABILITY

Limited liability arrives in Britain for companies, ultimately insulating those who run companies from the consequences of their actions. Company directors' liability is limited to any initial investments only. Philosophically, it gives companies—abstract legal entities—some of the same rights as ordinary people, but without the same responsibilities.

DAS KAPITAL

Karl Marx publishes *Das Kapital*, in social sciences still the most commonly cited book written before 1950. Marx criticizes capitalism as a model in which surplus value, taken as profit, results from the unpaid work, or exploitation, of the labor force. A solution is for workforces to "own the means of production."

1947

NEOLIBERALISM

Milton Friedman, Friedrich von Hayek, Ludvig von Mises, and others gather at Mont Pèlerin to oppose ideas that emphasize common purpose and governments acting directly in the economy for public interest. They aim to marry old, neoclassical beliefs in deregulated markets with liberal concerns about personal freedom.

1961

DECOLONIZATION

Frantz Fanon publishes *The Wretched of the Earth*, capturing the spirit of an era of decolonization, as new approaches to independent economic development emerge after World War II, replacing the European colonialism that has previously legitimized the exploitation of peoples and natural resources.

2008

LEHMAN BROTHERS

The investment company Lehman Brothers collapses shortly after announcing losses of nearly $4 billion, having driven the growth in subprime mortgage lending. This leads directly to the collapse of other banks around the world, bailed out by their governments, terrified of a repeat of the Lehman experience.

BIOGRAPHIES

ADAM SMITH (1723–1790)

The political economist and moral philosopher Adam Smith entered the University of Glasgow at the age of 14, then was awarded a scholarship to Oxford University. Eventually returning to Scotland, he joined a circle of thinkers that included David Hume and David Ricardo. Smith remains perhaps the most recognized and controversial figure in the history of Western economic thought. His ideas emerged out of the Scottish Enlightenment and led to the unraveling of the prevailing "mercantile" approach to economics. He is seen as the grandfather of market economics, but his works *The Theory of Moral Sentiments* (1759) and *The Wealth of Nations* (1776) reveal a more complex thinker than he is often thought to be. He is famous for the "invisible hand"—the idea that self-interest and unmanaged markets work best—and the example of the manufacture of the pin, revealing how the specialization and division of labor leads to huge increases in productivity. But Smith also warned about the dehumanizing effects of specialization, was critical of consumerism, warned about the power of corporations, and emphasized the important role of the state in maintaining public institutions and services, and protecting society from injustice and oppression.

JEREMY BENTHAM (1748–1832)

The English social reformer and pioneering utilitarian philosopher Jeremy Bentham also had a great deal to say about economics—mainly as an advocate for expanding the money supply to create full employment. But it was his utilitarianism that has had the greatest influence for the man who left his preserved skeleton as a memorial to University College London. Bentham proposed that the measure of all morality should be a mathematical calculation of "the greatest good of the greatest number." It was this that has led to him being the founder of social welfare. There are obvious objections to utilitarianism as a moral philosophy—given that few of us whip out the calculator to work out what is right or wrong—but it is a useful rule of thumb in public policy, and here Bentham was a real pioneer. He opposed slavery, and the death penalty and physical punishment, especially of children. He called for rights for women and homosexuals, a better separation between Church and State, and freedom of expression. In that respect, he was one of the founding fathers of modern liberalism, and also of modernism as a political philosophy.

MARY PALEY MARSHALL (1850–1944)

Mary Paley, a relation of the utilitarian philosopher William Paley, was the coauthor with Alfred Marshall of *The Economics of History*. (Alfred was Mary's tutor, and later her husband.) Mary was taught science and mathematics by her father, Reverend Thomas Paley, who ensured that her education carried on beyond the age of 13, when it typically stopped for girls. After successfully taking a teaching exam, Mary became one of the first women undergraduates accepted at Cambridge University, and deeply impressed the great economist John Maynard Keynes. Ironically, her husband campaigned actively against women being educated at university. Although receiving the highest mark in her course on the moral sciences, Mary was denied a degree because she was a woman, but she went on to lecture in economics at what later became Newnham College. Her teaching was published in 1879 as *The Economics of Industry* (pictured below). Mary is also widely believed to have contributed significantly to *Principles of Economics*, published in 1890 under Alfred Marshall's name, a work that defined neoclassical economics and became a standard textbook for generations of students.

THE

ECONOMICS OF INDUSTRY

BY

ALFRED MARSHALL,

AND

MARY PALEY MARSHALL,

ROSA LUXEMBURG (1871–1919)

Rosa Luxemburg was an influential Polish, Marxist economist and philosopher, and one of few women to gain a doctorate in the nineteenth century—in law and political economy, from the University of Zurich. As an activist from school days, she emigrated to Switzerland to avoid potential imprisonment. Opposed to nationalisms of all kinds, she campaigned for internationalism based on socialism, and rejected gradual or "reformist" approaches to change as doomed to being coopted, arguing instead for the need for revolution. Luxemburg wrote about the economic development of Poland and was fiercely critical of capitalism in her work *The Accumulation of Capital: A Contribution to an Economic Explanation of Imperialism*. But she was also extremely critical of others on the Left, advocating a strongly democratic and decentralized form of socialism. Popular again today, her letters are still widely read and admired. In them she reveals a deeply poetic appreciation of life and, many decades before the publication of Rachel Carson's *Silent Spring* (1962), an awareness and sorrow over the environmental impact of industry and industrial farming.

THE INVISIBLE HAND

THE MAIN CONCEPT | Possibly the single most influential idea in modern economics, the metaphor of the invisible hand was introduced by Adam Smith in his seminal *Wealth of Nations*. "The rich," he wrote, "are led by an invisible hand . . . and thus without intending it, without knowing it, advance the interest of the society." Smith believed that the general interest of society would best be served in a market place with minimal rules and regulations: the overall outcome of self-interested transactions by multiple players and not the specific intention of any one player. Because of the way that businesses compete for advantage, innovating and lowering prices, equilibrium would naturally be found between the level of demand and supply. This would result in resources being distributed with the greatest efficiency. Smith's famous example of one way in which this might happen concerned the manufacture of a pin. Instead of one individual performing multiple tasks, by breaking the manufacture down into separate elements—the specialization and division of labor—there would be huge increases in productivity and competitive advantage through lower prices. Smith believed that nothing should obstruct the pursuit of self-interest because it would prevent markets working efficiently.

DRILL DOWN | Smith also presented the human cost of an economy in the grip of the invisible hand. The monotony of divided, specialized work would lead, he said, to the worker no longer being able to "exert his understanding" and becoming "stupid and ignorant." There was also a danger that whenever traders got together it would lead to a "conspiracy against the public, or in some contrivance to raise prices." The state, Smith said, had a duty to protect society from violence, to protect every member from "the injustice or oppression of every other member," and critically, to "erect and maintain those public institutions and those public works" that although vital to society are not profitable, so of no interest to private enterprise.

MERCANTILISM
Page 26
CLASSICAL ECONOMICS
Page 28
PRODUCTIVITY
Page 58

FOCUS | *Economics, dubbed the "dismal science," is not famously full of jokes, but one goes . . . Question: How many neoliberal economists does it take to change a light bulb? Answer: None. They sit in the dark and wait for the invisible hand of the market to do it.*

UTILITY & RATIONAL ECONOMIC MAN

THE MAIN CONCEPT | The English philosopher Jeremy Bentham said that utility was the principle on which things are judged according to their ability "to augment or diminish the happiness of the party whose interest is in question." Mainstream economics says that we are primarily and rationally motivated to maximize this utility. However, we often lack sufficient information to make such calculating choices and are more strongly swayed by emotion, bias, or incidental details. Another consideration is how we measure success. Economists think this can be done by looking at our "expressed preferences"—what we buy. This leaves us with a system where we do more to augment our happiness by buying drain cleaner than by strolling through sun-dappled woodlands. Real life is also full of examples of people making choices that are neither rational nor maximize their utility. For example, we may go shopping in the belief that acquiring new goods will make us happy, yet we end up dissatisfied and wanting the next thing—in other words, being stuck on the "hedonic treadmill." We are influenced by fashion, the choices of others, habit, and addictive behaviors—which can reduce rather than add to our happiness and well-being. All of these factors color what are theoretically rational choices.

DRILL DOWN | A quirk of this system, is its way of measuring success, with the assumption that the more we spend, the more we acquire, and the happier we are. It doesn't take much to realize that bizarre anomalies can arise as a result of these goals. In Costa Rica, the amount spent on goods and services per person is only one-fifth of the amount spent in the United States. So, does that mean that in the US, by making rational choices, people achieve five times more utility, happiness, and well-being? No. In fact, both well-being and life expectancy are lower in the US, and use of natural resources is three times higher per person than in Costa Rica.

NEW ECONOMIC INDICATORS
Page 102

WELL-BEING
Page 106

GROWTH & DEVELOPMENT
Page 134

FOCUS | *Economics has a term for those things we buy that can undermine our well-being, such as drugs or excess alcohol—"demerit goods." Other exotic terms to describe behavior that doesn't fit with the mainstream theory include: "irrational exuberance," when the herd behavior of speculators raises something's value far beyond realistic assessment, and "sunk-cost fallacy," when you've already invested so much in a thing that you keep doing so even when it's a lost cause.*

PRODUCTIVITY

THE MAIN CONCEPT | Productivity, like growth, is one of the bellwethers of conventional measures of economic success. Having fewer people produce more is seen as a fundamental efficiency from which a rise in living standards can flow. But in a world in which paid employment is seen as an essential part of citizenship, rising productivity can create its own problems. The same expectations cannot be brought to all sectors of the economy. Some, by their nature, have greater potential to increase productivity than others. Take mechanization: the costs of labor are lowered by replacing people with machines. But if human contact is at the heart of a job—as it is with a teacher, speech therapist, or nurse—it is harder to raise productivity. This leads to a common problem that economist William Baumol identified, now known as "Baumol's cost disease." This is where it is harder to reduce costs in certain—often public—sectors, such as health and education, because the nature of that work is less prone to the kind of mechanization that more easily raises productivity in manufacturing, for example. Baumol explained that this comes from unrealistic expectations. Take a class of 30 seven-year-olds, increase the class size to 50, then perhaps replace their teacher with a video link to a remote teacher speaking to many classes at the same time. This wouldn't be an increase in productivity, but a bad education system.

DRILL DOWN | In capitalist economies, investors demand more from less. If a factory employing ten people produces 100 widgets in one year, the next year investors might expect the production of more widgets, say 108. But, what happens if there are environmental limits, and to produce more than 100 widgets a year would be unsustainable? And if nothing else changed, in order to get the expected return on investment, the 100 widgets would have to cost less to produce, and so be the work of only nine people, and so on. An endlessly expanding economy can mask this problem simply by having more people producing ever more goods and services.

FOCUS | *Baumol gave the famous example that while many things may have changed in the last 200 years, a Mozart string quartet still requires the same number of players and the same amount of time that it did when first performed in the eighteenth century. There are limits to productivity.*

SOCIAL CAPITAL
Page 98

NEW ECONOMIC INDICATORS
Page 102

THE ECONOMICS OF SCALE
Page 132

MACROECONOMICS & MICROECONOMICS

THE MAIN CONCEPT | One of the most common distinctions in the field of economics is between macro- and microeconomics—terms coined by a Norwegian economist, Ragnar Frisch, in 1933. As the names suggest, these two approaches to understanding the economy focus on big things and small things. Macroeconomics is concerned with what happens in the economy at the scale of large variables interacting with each other, such as employment, inflation, and total production and growth. Similarly, macroeconomic policy tools operate at the economy-wide level of tax and government spending. Controlling the amount of money in circulation is another mechanism, manipulated through interest rates and how much money banks are allowed to create—through lending for mortgages, for example—relative to their reserves of capital. Microeconomics, conversely, studies the behavior of individuals, families, businesses, and particular markets. Policies are concerned with influencing behavior at these levels with a variety of incentives and penalties, and might include changes in the regulatory environment for businesses. Microeconomics also looks at shifts in taxes and rates, competition policy (how much of a market one or a few firms are allowed to control), or decisions on the ownership of parts of the economy through models such as privatization, nationalization, or mutualization.

DRILL DOWN | The reputation of macroeconomics for economic forecasting suffered greatly in the crisis of 2007–8, which only a handful of mostly marginalized economists saw coming. Prominent investors have also declared macroeconomics almost useless as a guide to individual investment decisions. With the rise of inequality, especially in the Anglo Saxon economies, the usefulness of microeconomics in guiding policy has been problematic, too. The introduction of a minimum wage, for example, though widely supported, is the wrong thing to do according to microeconomics, since it disrupts classic demand and supply. It raises costs to employers, so "should" reduce employment. Yet, the evidence is mixed, and regardless, if the market is producing levels of inequality that are generally considered "wrong," there are other legitimate reasons to stray from the theory.

CREDIT & DEBT
Page 24
PRODUCTIVITY
Page 58
BEHAVIORAL ECONOMICS
Page 88

FOCUS | *The irony of macroeconomics is that it has no theory of "optimal scale"—how large an economy should be. Microeconomics, on the other hand, deals with the practicalities of households and firms, but typically relies on abstract models rather than real economic circumstances to understand them. As economist and standup comedian Yoram Bauman quipped—"microeconomists are wrong about specific things, whereas macroeconomists are wrong in general."*

DEMAND & SUPPLY

THE MAIN CONCEPT | In a consumer society, demand—a consumer's desire to pay for something—rules, and it needs suppliers. The ideal is to have the two meet in a way that makes both feel that they are getting a good deal. In a competitive market, this equilibrium is found when the amounts of something demanded and supplied become equal at a certain price. This assumes that suppliers will keep producing a good for as long as their costs are below the price they can get for it. As economic success is often defined by growth, more demand is generally considered a good thing, while weak demand may lead to recession. Conversely, too much demand chasing too few goods and services can drive up prices. The expectation is that demand lowers as price rises. But this is not a simple relationship. Where a rise in price strongly reduces demand for a good, it is said to be "elastic." But with goods such as tobacco or business flights, where consumers' purchases are also dictated by powerful habits or social norms, the demand is said to be a lot more "inelastic"—raising the price is less likely significantly to alter the quantities purchased. In reality, where suppliers have control of a market, and regulation is weak, they have the power to set prices.

DRILL DOWN | When suppliers are unable to provide something at a price on which buyer and seller can agree, it leads to "unmet demand," a problem that in theory shouldn't exist. The failure of some privatized services like care homes and rail franchises illustrates this. And yet, the notion that demand should be managed in any other way is often seen as an unacceptable intervention in the market. But limits sometimes do need to be put on consumption. Take fossil fuels: price alone cannot guarantee limits on their use; to meet agreed international emission targets, there is no price at which an unsafe amount of fossil fuels should be bought and burned.

THE INVISIBLE HAND
Page 54

INFLATION
Page 64

PRICE
Page 66

FOCUS | *During its 1846–52 famine, which, combined with disease, killed around one million people, Ireland under British rule continued to export a wide range of food, from grain to livestock. The same thing has occurred in many famines since. Political and economic failings often mean demand and available supply do not meet, with fatal consequences.*

INFLATION

THE MAIN CONCEPT | Inflation might not seem like a big idea, but simply the description of a rise in the general level of prices over time, and yet the position it holds in the imagination of policy makers and the economic mainstream makes it a big idea. Inflation typically results from too much money chasing too few goods. A fear of inflation means that most major economies have policies to rigidly control it, typically setting very low targets to allow a rise in prices of a couple of percent at most. There are two obvious reasons for this. Firstly, large and sustained increases in prices lower the purchasing power of money, meaning that people can buy less with their money and that the value of savings falls. Politicians are always keen to avoid this scenario, for fear of the backlash from electorates. Their other fear is that high inflation will encourage workforces to demand pay raises, increasing costs to employers in both the public and private sector. In extreme circumstances there is the danger of a "wages—prices spiral." There is also the threat of runaway inflation, or "hyperinflation," famously experienced in Germany between the two world wars, and in Zimbabwe between 2007 and 2008. Hyperinflation can leave countries almost ungovernable.

DRILL DOWN | Since the financial crisis of 2007–8, economists such as Paul Krugman have argued that economies face a bigger problem with deflation—a continual fall in prices—than inflation. With deflation people stop spending, less money circulates, jobs are lost, and an economy may grind to a halt. Instead of austerity measures such as cuts in public spending, there should, Krugman argues, be an emphasis on public spending. Rather than creating public debt, this would have a multiplier effect, triggering economic activity and hence tax receipts. Krugman advocates for focusing public investment where there is a need, demand, and a growing market—such as the switch to a low-carbon economy.

FOCUS | *In May 1991, Norman Lamont (Chancellor of the Exchequer of Margaret Thatcher's Conservative government in the UK), notoriously said, "Rising unemployment and the recession have been the price that we have had to pay to get inflation down," adding, "That price is well worth paying." It was a quote that quickly entered the history books.*

KEYNESIAN ECONOMICS
Page 36

PRICE
Page 66

GRESHAM'S LAW
Page 92

PRICE

THE MAIN CONCEPT | Price may appear to be something technical, rather than a big idea, but it is one of mainstream economics' biggest ideas, and one of its most controversial. A price is what you pay, in money, in return for a good or a service. Prices are meant to be located where the lines on the graph of demand and supply intersect. But rather than following the theory of perfect competitive equilibrium, the reality of how prices get set in markets is much more messy and varied. Often prices are established using "cost-plus pricing," where the cost of producing a good is used as the basis, and a markup for profit is added. Prices can also be the result of unspoken agreements in markets with a few dominant players, where prices are set in reference to each other at "coincidentally" similar levels. For sectors that experience huge variations in demand at different times—such as transportation services for commuters, or hotels during vacation periods—algorithms are used both to even out demand and to profit during times of peak usage. Economies as a whole rely on the signal sent by prices to allocate scarce resources efficiently and to ensure that markets meet people's needs. A price is also meant to contain all the information you need to make the best decisions. But in practice, prices often don't carry vital information, such as the human cost of production, the impact on human health of consumption, or future environmental damage.

DRILL DOWN | If someone was planning to build on a meadow that you cared for, you could be asked two questions: How much would you pay to save it? Or how much compensation would you demand for its loss? Two very different prices would result—one constrained by the ability to pay; the other perhaps infinitely high. Prices are not just points on demand and supply graphs, but judgments of value. In a misguided early attempt to assess both the likely costs of climate change and the benefits of action to stop it, in a 1995 draft report of the Intergovernmental Panel on Climate Change, economists suggested that the price of a human life was 15 times higher in rich countries than in poor countries, causing huge controversy.

FOCUS | *Vera Coking bought a house in Atlantic City, New Jersey, in 1961 for $20,000. When she was offered $1 million for the property by Bob Guccione, owner of* Penthouse *magazine, who wanted to build a hotel and casino on the site, she refused. In 1993 she also refused Donald Trump, who wanted the land for a parking lot for limousines for his nearby casino and hotel, which went out of business in 2014.*

UTILITY & RATIONAL ECONOMIC MAN
Page 56

DEMAND & SUPPLY
Page 62

INFLATION
Page 64

COMPARATIVE ADVANTAGE

THE MAIN CONCEPT | The imperative of free trade has been the hallmark of globalization for the last half century, and trade as a share of economic activity has grown enormously. The idea that large-scale trade would bring about general gain can be traced to the idea of comparative advantage, promoted by David Ricardo in his 1817 book *On the Principles of Political Economy and Taxation*. This proposes that countries should specialize in goods for which they have the lowest opportunity cost (the cost of choosing one thing over another). The classic example was trade between Britain and Portugal, countries that had the ability to make both textiles and wine. Instead of making and trading both, Ricardo argued that there would be a benefit to both if each specialized in the product that they lost least by concentrating on. Britain would be better off foregoing the making of wine to focus on cloth manufacture, importing wine from Portugal instead, which enjoyed a comparative advantage in winemaking; Portugal would be better off sticking to wine and importing cloth from Britain. The complication, however, is that countries are always at different stages of development. They may find themselves concentrating on low-value commodities—and end up specializing in being poor.

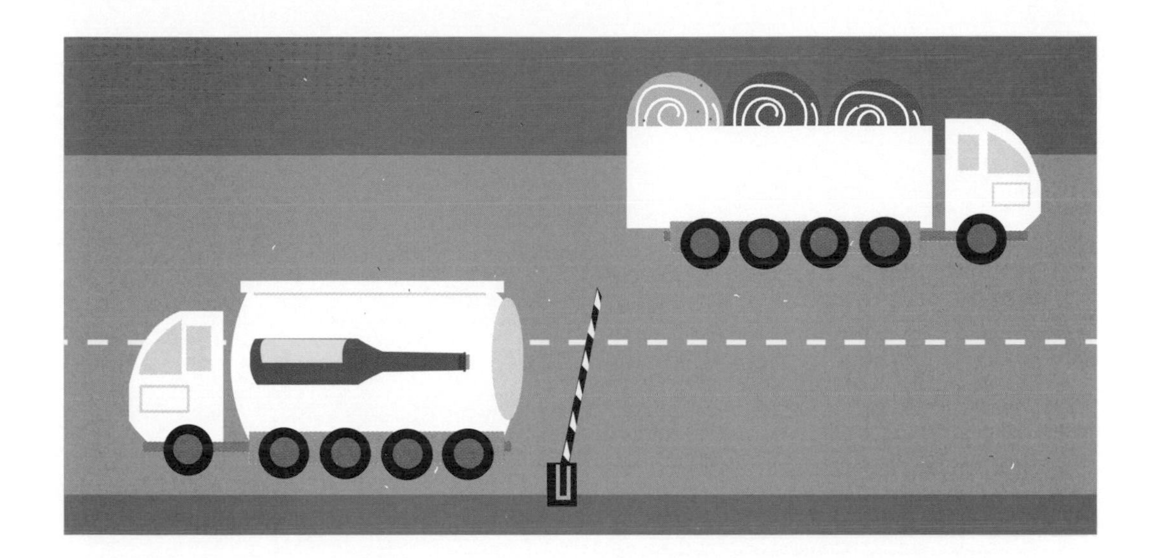

DRILL DOWN | Before Ricardo and other advocates of free trade, the notion that a general struggle for gain might bind a community together would have seemed like madness. Both the US and the UK employed multiple protectionist measures to establish their dominance before preaching free trade to the world. As the economist Dani Rodrik observed, "US import tariffs during the latter half of the nineteenth century were higher than in all but a few developing countries today." Worse still, wrote Mike Davis, "every serious attempt by a non-Western society to . . . regulate its terms of trade was met by a military as well as an economic response from London or a competing imperial capital."

FOCUS | *The trade economist Paul Krugman wrote of a "dirty little secret" in the analysis of international trade—one that hides the fact that the costs of protectionism "are not all that large," while the "empirical evidence" of the great benefits of liberalization "is at best fuzzy." And leading economist Ha-Joon Chang notes that Asian economies like South Korea and Taiwan enjoyed rapid development while rejecting the ideologies of free trade and free capital movement.*

MERCANTILISM
Page 26

CLASSICAL ECONOMICS
Page 28

GLOBALIZATION
Page 40

MONETARISM

THE MAIN CONCEPT | Coined by neoliberal economist Milton Friedman in 1967, monetarism is the school of economic thought that believes that the amount of money in the economy—the so-called money supply—is the key determinant of growth. But, it is not simply that a bigger supply is meant to be better. Monetarists fear inflation if too much money is in circulation, while too little money circulating creates unemployment, so they seek a "Goldilocks" economy with just the right amount, and emphasize the use of interest rates to control this. Higher rates of interest encourage people to save more and borrow less. Monetarism, though, is contentious, and one of the most politicized of all economic theories because of its association with the right-wing administrations of Margaret Thatcher and Ronald Reagan in the late 1970s and 1980s. Controversially, it was used as part of an argument for minimizing the direct role of government in economic management, and to argue against public spending, seen as a poorly targeted and potentially inflationary way of boosting the money supply and stimulating the economy. In this scenario, central banks, which control interest rates but are not democratically accountable, become potentially more powerful than governments.

DRILL DOWN | The great criticism of monetarism is that it is demand for goods and services, not the money supply, that drives output levels. When Chairman Paul Volcker used monetarist policies at the US Federal Reserve in 1979 to control inflation, he was successful, but he also caused a recession. Monetarism was seen to have a fatal flaw—it relied on a stable, predictable relationship between money and economic output. In reality, money circulates at an unpredictable speed, and in an increasingly financialized economy, with complex automated trading, volatility increases, which renders money supply useless as a policy target. In 2014 even the International Monetary Fund came to the conclusion that monetarism didn't work.

FOCUS | *The American writer Gore Vidal once described the American economic system as "free enterprise for the poor and socialism for the rich." Macroeconomic policy on the global scale is a bit like that. "It is Keynesianism for the rich countries and monetarism for the poor," wrote economist Ha-Joon Chang in* Bad Samaritans *(2007).*

CENTRAL BANKS
Page 30
KEYNESIAN ECONOMICS
Page 36
THE RISE OF THE QUANTS
Page 44

ECONOMIC CYCLES

THE MAIN CONCEPT | You will often hear commentators talking about economic cycles, but there are in fact several distinct but interacting types, including business, market, and debt cycles. Business cycles comprise the rise and fall of output across an entire economy; market cycles describe the rise and fall in the value of stock markets; and debt cycles record the rise and fall in levels of debt held by governments and households. In popular economic debate, economic cycles are often discussed in terms of boom and bust—periods of rapidly increasing economic activity and/or share value, before a crash or period of stasis or decline. Several attempts have been made to describe the regularity of economic cycles. In 1860, the French statistician Clément Juglar identified a cycle of around 8 to 11 years—known as the "Juglar cycle." Then in 1930, the American economist Simon Kuznets identified the "Kuznets swing," a cycle of 15 to 25 years, shaped by waves of investment in infrastructure. But perhaps the best-known description of a cycle is the "Kondratiev wave." Russian economist Nikolai Kondratiev believed that an economic cycle spanned 45 to 60 years, dictated by technological innovation. However, rejecting the idea that economies were inherently stable, Karl Marx proposed that industrial capitalism would be prone to increasingly severe crises until it brought about its own complete downfall.

DRILL DOWN | Gordon Brown, the UK's Chancellor of the Exchequer from 1997 to 2007, was committed to a "Britain where there is not stop go and boom bust but economic stability," and introduced the setting of interest rates by an independent Monetary Policy Committee. On the financial sector, he said in 2006, "Many who advised me . . . favored a regulatory crackdown. I believe that we were right not to go down that road." In spring 2007 he promised, "we will never return to the old boom and bust." Financial services would help "secure our place in the high value-added, investment-driven growth sectors of the future." A few months later the UK experienced one of its biggest crashes for decades.

FOCUS | *The Bank of England's Andrew Haldane estimated that the cost of the 2007–8 crisis to the UK economy alone was between £1.8 trillion and £7.4 trillion ($2.3–9.4 trillion). "To call these numbers 'astronomical,' he said, "would be to do astronomy a disservice: there are only hundreds of billions of stars in the galaxy."*

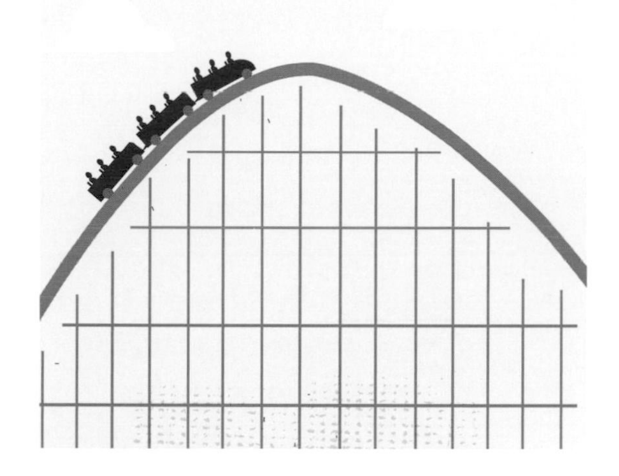

CREDIT & DEBT
Page 24

GREAT BUBBLES & CRASHES
Page 34

INFLATION
Page 64

MONOPOLIES

THE MAIN CONCEPT | Monopolies are news again. From the days of Adam Smith to the rise of the railroads in the United States, the threat of monopolies was a major concern of regulators. Tough antimonopoly, or “antitrust,” action was taken, which attempted to guarantee open markets and consumer choice, and prevent tyrannical corporations from cornering the market. Presidents like Theodore Roosevelt and William Taft led the antitrust push in the early twentieth century, breaking up monopolies and oligopolies like John Rockefeller’s Standard Oil. Then a shift in thinking raised a new question: did they really matter? In 1962, Milton Friedman wrote in *Capitalism and Freedom* that monopolies were rarely a problem and, when they were, it was normally the fault of governments. During the Reagan years, the conservative lawyer Robert Bork argued in *The Anti-Trust Paradox* (1978) that concerns about monopolies were trumped by the need for economies of scale (the savings made when production is scaled up). Now the pendulum has swung again. From pharmaceuticals to food, and retail to banking, power is being concentrated into ever fewer hands across the economy, challenging regulators to act in the public interest on grounds of tax, privacy, and choice.

DRILL DOWN | The problem with economies of scale is that they are often overtaken by the "diseconomies" of scale, one of which is the inefficiencies of monopolistic companies, and the way they begin to lose interest in their own customers' needs. Recent research suggests that the gap between prices and costs is now much wider (67 percent) and that the proportion of GDP spent on investment is also falling. Neither of these problems is restricted to monopolies, but they are certainly what you might expect if monopolies were a problem. There is also rising political concern about this issue on both sides of the Atlantic, so watch this space!

THE CHICAGO SCHOOL
Page 38

COMPARATIVE ADVANTAGE
Page 68

THE ECONOMICS OF SCALE
Page 132

FOCUS | *While ever fewer, larger corporations are controlling bigger shares of the economy, key regulators have become less active, as shown by the investigations carried out by the US Department of Trade into abuses of monopoly power. In 1994, they launched 22 investigations, but 20 years later, in 2014, they launched none at all.*

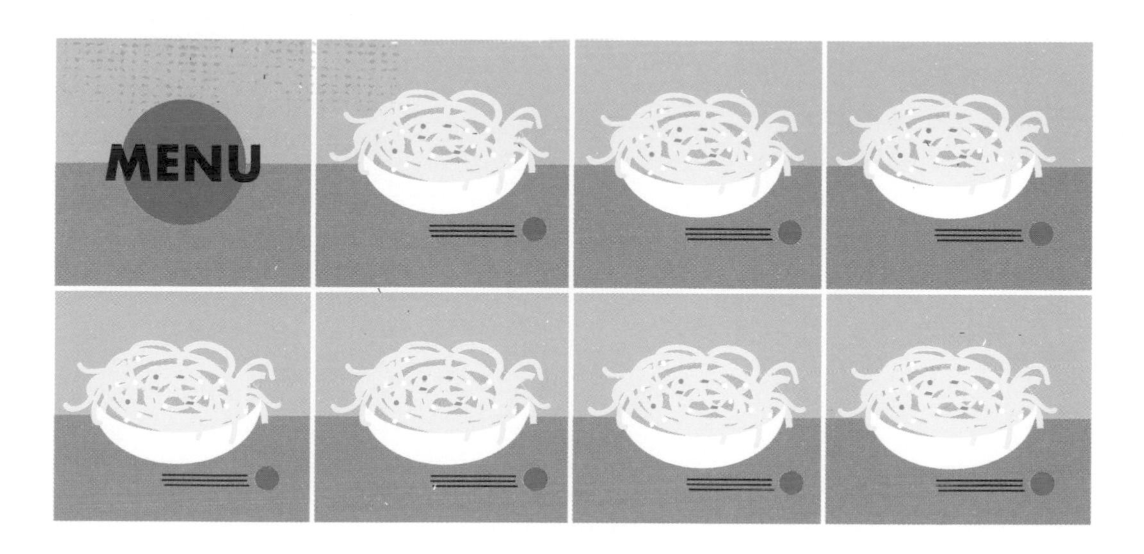

COMPLEXITY

THE MAIN CONCEPT | The world is too complicated to be described meaningfully by standard economic models. That is the claim made by the emerging discipline of complexity economics. As US economist W. Brian Arthur has noted, in viewing the economy not as something "given" but which "forms from a constantly developing set of institutions, arrangements, and technological innovations," it is closer in spirit to political economy. Following this interpretation of the economy as dynamic and evolutionary, the complexity school of thought rejects the notion of a system in equilibrium. Whereas standard economic models rely heavily upon simplifying assumptions in order to find a best-fit theory, complexity economics treats the world as a complex, adaptive, and interdependent system. It draws on complexity theory, which itself combines insights from cognitive psychology, evolutionary biology, chaos, information, and general systems theory, and other disciplines. As a new tool for economists, it may help explain things that catch many of them by surprise, such as the subprime mortgage crisis that triggered the financial collapse of 2007–8. According to David Viniar, then Chief Financial Officer of Goldman Sachs, the risk of what actually happened at the height of the crisis was a so-called "25 sigma"—in other words, effectively impossible.

DRILL DOWN | A collaboration between the former UK government Chief Scientific Advisor Robert May and the Bank of England's Andrew Haldane aimed to understand economic phenomena through insights from other complex systems. They compared food webs and contagious diseases to the malfunctioning of financial markets. Before the 2007–8 crisis, "an increasingly elaborate set of financial instruments emerged, intended to optimize returns to individual institutions with seemingly minimal risk . . ." but, "Essentially no attention was given to their possible effects on the stability of the system as a whole." The growth, concentration, and complexity of the banking sector had analogies with instability in ecological food webs; meanwhile certain banks were like "super spreaders" of disease.

CENTRAL BANKS
Page 30
THE RISE OF THE QUANTS
Page 44
EFFICIENT MARKETS
Page 78

FOCUS | *The notional value of increasingly complex derivatives—contracts between parties whose value is based on an underlying asset—rose over the course of a decade from 1998, from under $100 trillion, to over $600 trillion. For comparison, the latter figure was about 39 times the size of the US economy in 2011.*

EFFICIENT MARKETS

THE MAIN CONCEPT | There are many ways in which neoclassical and neoliberal economic theory promote the supposed efficiency of markets. Devised in the 1960s by economist Eugene Fama, the "efficient market hypothesis" proposed that it was literally impossible to "beat the market"—the price mechanism was so effective that it would already carry all the necessary information that might influence the price of a financial product or the share price of a company. Others argue that financial markets are shaped by bias, herd behavior, subjective expectations, projections based on past performance, overconfidence, and overreaction. Investors such as Warren Buffet dispute the efficient market hypothesis; others like Jeremy Grantham claim that it led to the 2007–8 financial crisis by leading to "a chronic under-estimation of the dangers of asset bubbles breaking" among regulators. Successive heads of the Federal Reserve, Alan Greenspan and Ben Bernanke, "were not sure that bubbles . . . could even exist." Beneath the surface of mainstream market economics these assumptions of the alleged efficiency of market systems strongly influence policy making, even if they are extreme simplifications not meant to be taken literally.

GREAT BUBBLES & CRASHES
Page 34
PRICE
Page 66
COMPLEXITY
Page 76

DRILL DOWN | The theory of perfect competition under perfect markets assumes that everybody has "perfect information" (knowing everything about what is bought and sold), and that there is "perfect competition" between an infinite number of firms—where there are no barriers to entering a market, firms cannot influence the price of goods, and all products are interchangeable. After the 2007–8 crisis, Alan Greenspan explained to a Senate committee, "I made a mistake in presuming that the self-interest of organizations, specifically banks, is such that they were best capable of protecting shareholders and equity in the firms," adding, "I discovered a flaw in the model that I perceived is the critical functioning structure that defines how the world works."

FOCUS | *Markets often fail due to weak regulation, and it keeps happening, because of a systemic problem. Writing on the 1929 Great Crash, Canadian economist John Kenneth Galbraith blamed the regulators' short life cycle, in which they are, "Vigorous in youth, rapidly turning complacent in middle age, before either becoming senile or an arm of the industry they are meant to regulate."*

"Financial capital— the wherewithal for mass marketing— has steadily replaced social capital—that is, grassroots citizen networks—as the coin of the realm."

ROBERT PUTNAM,
BOWLING ALONE (2000)

3 ECONOMICS & PEOPLE

INTRODUCTION

"It was in the beginning a modest initiative, almost confidential," wrote the French newspaper *Le Monde* in September 2000. "It has now become a subject of an important debate which has created a state of effervescence in the community of economists. Should not the teaching of economics in universities be re-thought?" They were talking about the new "post-autistic economics" revolt at the Sorbonne in Paris, where a small group of students had protested on the Web against the "uncontrolled use of mathematics" in economics. They claimed that mathematics had "become an end in itself," turning economics into what they called an "autistic science," dominated by abstractions that bore too little relation to the real world.

By the fall, the campaign had led to a major debate at the Sorbonne, and the French education minister, Jack Lang, had promised to set up a commission to investigate the situation and come up with some proposals to change economics teaching. Economists pointed out at the time that they knew perfectly well that their formulae and abstract models did not always fit the real world. The issue has been what should be done about that—how do we bring people, with all their variety and contradictions, back into the picture? That is what this chapter is all about.

Economics for the real world

The revolt of economics students continued to spread, especially after the financial crisis of 2007–8, and there is now growing interest in how the discipline can take better account of the way human beings are in the real world. We therefore begin this chapter with an entry on behavioral economics (pages 88–89), which describes the alliance between economists and psychologists to look at how people behave in reality rather than in theory. This discipline has provided us with some cutting-edge insights into modern economics.

Theories about labor and the lump of labor fallacy (pages 90–91)—the hypothesis that, in practice, it is not possible to spread work out equally between workers, much as it might make sense to do so—goes back to previous eras of economics, for example, in the days of Karl Marx, when labor was one of a trio of capitals (alongside land and finance) required to produce wealth.

The central idea of this chapter is that theoretical models do not always describe the real world, any more than common sense theories always do. That is certainly the idea behind the inclusion of an entry on Gresham's law (pages 92–93), named after an Elizabethan financier who noticed that bad money—the stuff nobody wants to save—tends to drive out the good money in circulation. This is followed by an entry on game theory (pages 94–95), which refers to the application of games to economics, and the market in particular—an approach that has gripped economic theorists over recent decades.

Considering the human dimension

The next six entries cover ideas that add a human dimension to economic theory. Institutional economics (pages 96–97) looks at the vital importance of institutions in successful economies. Social capital (pages 98–99) looks at the fundamental issue of human relations. Intellectual capital (pages 100–101) discusses the critical role played by knowledge in the creation of wealth. New economic indicators (pages 102–3) looks at broader ways of measuring success than simply in terms of money. New kinds of money (pages 104–5) then broadens this theme by looking at how these different measures might be turned into money, and with the same kinds of functions as money. Finally, an entry on well-being (pages 106–7) looks at one new economic indicator in particular—assuming that behind financial wealth lies something that may be valued more by people in practice.

The final three entries in this chapter all touch upon further human dimensions of economic theory—feminist economics (pages 108–9) looks at some of these issues from the point of view of women, the core economy (pages 110–11) investigates them from the point of view of the local community, and the sharing economy (pages 112–13) from the point of view of cooperative enterprises.

Taken together, the approach of this chapter is to look at "economics as if people mattered," to quote the subtitle of Fritz Schumacher's best-selling green manual *Small is Beautiful* (1973). More then four decades on, it is clear that economics itself is beginning to adapt so that they do.

TIMELINE

ILLUSTRATIONS OF POLITICAL ECONOMY

The polymath Harriet Martineau—a key figure in theological circles, a pioneering sociologist, and a best-selling author of economics in popular form—publishes her *Illustrations*. This merges fiction and economics to demonstrate economic types and theories.

THE NEW DEAL

Franklin Roosevelt takes office in March 1933, at the height of the Great Depression, when a quarter of all US banks have closed their doors. The New Deal is his initial emergency response—a series of federal agencies who are tasked to provide paid work for farm workers, the young, and the old.

1934

NATIONAL ACCOUNTS

American economist Simon Kuznets takes charge of the project to look at how to estimate the accounts of a nation in 1931, producing the first US national income accounts three years later. Related ideas are used to work out how to maximize the productivity of the economy, possibly playing a key role in winning World War II.

1990

BOWLING ALONE

Socio-economist Robert Putnam publishes his book on social capital, changing views on how social structures can influence economics. His title is taken from a visit to a bowling alley in Connecticut, where he witnesses isolated men—apparently with few or no friends—staring sadly up at the TV screens.

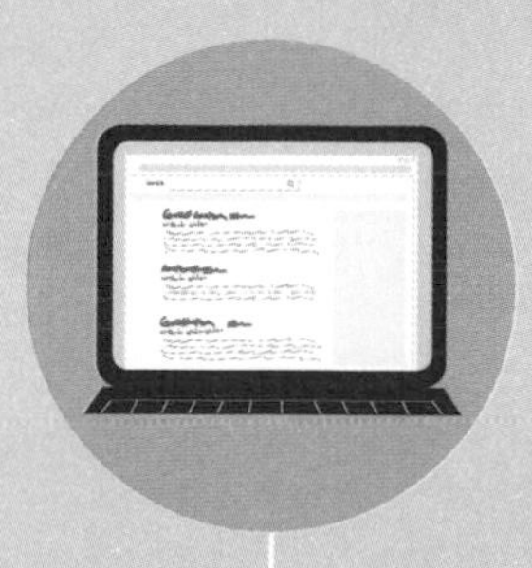

DOT-COM CRASH

The tech stocks phenomenon of the late 1990s has all the characteristics of a classic bubble: a technological development that will completely remake the economy, and doubters ridiculed in the press. A few e-commerce companies survive the crash—Amazon, eBay, Lastminute.com, and a few others—but the rest are swept away.

2000

POST-AUTISTIC ECONOMICS

A group of economics students at the Sorbonne in Paris claim that economics has become an abstract business of formulae and statistics—an "autistic science" that is dominated by mathematical abstractions that bear little relation to the real world.

2009

BITCOIN

A mysterious unknown person, or group of people, calling themselves Satoshi Nakamoto releases open-source cryptocurrency "bitcoin." This records transactions on a "blockchain," which is distributed widely around the world, rather than relying on issue by a central bank.

2009

ELINOR OSTROM

Elinor Ostrom becomes the only woman so far to win the Nobel Prize in Economics. The prize is awarded for her work on cooperative and informal systems of managing scarce planetary resources, which Ostrom shows are more effective than either privatization or central control by the state.

BIOGRAPHIES

THORSTEIN VEBLEN (1857–1929)

Thorstein Veblen is best known as the author of the influential 1899 book *The Theory of the Leisure Class*. He was born in Wisconsin after his family had arrived in the US from Norway with no English and very little money. The book provided us with the phrase "conspicuous consumption" and it was a sociological idea as much as an economic one. His idea was that the leisure classes bought products not because they were useful, but because they demonstrated their social status—which meant that those lower down the social hierarchy would then copy them. It has been hugely influential on socialist thinking. But Veblen was also the father of what has become known as "institutional economics," which shows the influence of evolutionary ideas, and which regards economic behavior as socially constructed and made possible by a succession of institutions, which have to evolve to keep their effectiveness. His 1904 book *The Theory of Business Enterprise* introduced the idea that has since become known as the "Veblenian dichotomy" between technology and the institutions that support its development and use, some of which are what Veblen called "ceremonial" (supporting social status) rather than useful.

JOSEPH SCHUMPETER (1883–1950)

Joseph Schumpeter was briefly Austrian finance minister in 1919, but is famous primarily as an economist at Harvard University, where he spent the rest of his career—and for his association with the phrase "creative destruction." This was, for him, the driver of capitalism, the gale of change that is brought by entrepreneurs, who are at the heart of his economics. Schumpeter's thinking provides some of the foundations of the ideas that have dominated the past four decades, but he also believed—like Karl Marx—that capitalism would inevitably collapse under the weight of its own contradictions. Schumpeter was also interested in economic cycles and popularized the 54-year cycles identified by Nikolai Kondratiev, though he is primarily known as one of the first innovation economists—as the first economist to look closely at the role of enterprise—and therefore one of the inspirations behind the heterodox economists, and thus, some of the ideas that this book relies on. Schumpeter declared that his purpose was to be the greatest economist in the world, the greatest horseman in Austria, and the greatest lover in Vienna—but that he had achieved only two of them. He never admitted which one he had failed to achieve.

ERNST FRIEDRICH SCHUMACHER (1911–1977)

The economist E. F. Schumacher was born in Germany and studied in his home country before moving to Oxford University in England, and then Columbia University in New York. He is regarded as the pioneering green economist, summed up in the subtitle of his highly influential 1973 book *Small Is Beautiful: A Study of Economics As If People Mattered*. Schumacher was not an environmental economist, the discipline devoted to pricing the environment into the economy, but fostered a far more radical critique, which began to emerge after a series of visits he made to Burma in the 1950s as an economic consultant. A former economist with the National Coal Board in the UK, Schumacher was lauded as a protégé by John Maynard Keynes. Schumacher proposed more democratic forms of company ownership and management, argued for the environmental limits to growth, took from Catholic teaching the principle of "subsidiarity"—economies being organized and decisions being taken at the most local practicable level—and advocated a more humanistic "Buddhist" economics.

MARILYN WARING (1953–)

Having graduated from the Victoria University of Wellington with a degree in political science and international politics two years previously, Marilyn Waring became the youngest MP in the New Zealand parliament when she was elected at the age of 23, and surprised everyone when—three years later—she was appointed to chair the Public Expenditure Committee. It was this experience that led her to delve more deeply into the way that women, their work, and their lives tended to be excluded from national accounting. Her findings were then recorded in her 1988 book *If Women Counted: A New Feminist Economics*, which would become one of the founding texts of feminist economics. Waring was truly an insider before authoring this book—not just chairing the Public Expenditure Committee, but also sitting on the board of the New Zealand central bank. Her decision to back a nuclear-free motion by the opposition brought down the conservative government of Robert Muldoon in 1984. Her work went on to influence the United Nations in the way they formulate economic statistics. Between research and public engagements, Waring also became a goat farmer.

BEHAVIORAL ECONOMICS

THE MAIN CONCEPT | Traditional economists have had to make certain psychological assumptions for their model to work—assumptions that a new breed of behavioral economists claim do not stand up. The theoretical construct at the heart of traditional economics, *Homo economicus*, is a rational person who takes decisions based on the broadest picture. It takes very little observation in the real world to find that this is hardly ever the case. Once you apply the lens of psychology to people's economic behavior you find, for example, that they are usually a good deal more scared of losing money than they are pleased at the prospect of gaining the same amount. Nor are they likely to dispose of cherished beliefs, despite the weight of evidence to the contrary. Habit matters, in other words. The popular book *Nudge* (2008), by Cass Sunstein and Richard Thaler, put behavioral economics firmly on the map, and important lessons have been learned, particularly in public policy. People now often have to opt out of their personal pension at work, rather than opting in; habit suggests that they may never actually opt in, even though it might be economically the best thing for them to do. The UK government even founded a (now independent) Nudge Unit to spread these practical policy design ideas.

DRILL DOWN | The behavioral economist Daniel Kahneman won the Nobel Prize in Economics for his work on what he and collaborator Amos Tversky called "prospect theory." This tried to model the otherwise peculiar way people take decisions based on risk—which has very little to do with actual probabilities. The difficulty with this and similar theories, however, is that it is simply based on observation. It relies on no psychological theory. It doesn't try to understand the way people behave—it simply tries to describe it, then converts it into the basis of a new economic model with graphs that make the same kind of assumptions about human beings that economic models do all too often. The basic assumption is that human beings are predictable machines.

FOCUS | *Economic theory suggests that more choice on the supermarket shelves, or anywhere else, is always a good thing. Not so, says Barry Schwartz in his influential book* The Paradox of Choice *(2004). According to Schwartz, too much choice makes consumers more anxious, an idea that flies in the face of economic tradition. In practice people want the right amount of choice for them.*

UTILITY & RATIONAL ECONOMIC MAN
Page 56

EFFICIENT MARKETS
Page 78

GAME THEORY
Page 94

THE WORKING WEEK

THE MAIN CONCEPT | The time we spend in formal employment is one of the sharpest realities of economic life that we face. Medieval workers apparently faced much shorter work hours (see page 23), while American author Barbara Ehrenreich wryly notes that in fifteenth-century France, one in every four days was an official holiday. J. M. Keynes famously believed that by now, with the logic of economic, social, and technological development, a 15-hour week would be common, with the rest of our time devoted to the art of living. It hasn't happened, but at least since the Industrial Revolution, the trajectory of history has been toward a shorter working week. The modern Saturday-to-Sunday weekend emerged gradually over the course of the twentieth century, often against resistance. The hours to be worked in a five-day week are still fought over. Increasingly, however, the argument is being made to continue the trend toward a shorter working week of three or four days to deliver a range of economic, social, and environmental benefits: redistributing available paid and unpaid work to broaden benefits, reduce inequalities, even out extremes of overwork and unemployment, improve the quality of family and civic life, and to free people from a consumer treadmill with its associated environmental impacts.

DRILL DOWN | An idea called the "lump of labor fallacy"—first suggested by US industrialists opposed to shorter work time—is often used against those advocating a week with fewer working days. What does it mean? Critics of shorter work time assume its advocates believe there is only a fixed amount of work available and say this is not true, as an expanding economy can always create more work. But even orthodox economics makes a case to control how long we work. In 1909 Sir Sydney Chapman argued that "competitive pressures" would result in the working week being so long that it would be counterproductive, and gave evidence that productivity improved after shorter working hours were introduced. In that case, reducing the hours worked can increase productivity, employment, and wages.

FOCUS | *In the Netherlands, workers can choose to work for fewer than five days a week. In 2008, in response to a funding crisis, the governor of Utah introduced a four-day week for nonemergency public workers—staff morale improved, absentee rates went down, a third of the public believed that services improved, and carbon emissions fell over six months by 14 percent. (Although successful, the scheme was suspended due to a change of administration.)*

MEDIEVAL ECONOMICS
Page 22

PRODUCTIVITY
Page 58

WELL-BEING
Page 106

GRESHAM'S LAW

THE MAIN CONCEPT | The phenomenon behind Gresham's law, that bad money tends to drive out good, was first noticed by one of Elizabeth I's courtiers, Sir Thomas Gresham. He observed that when the government introduced new currency into circulation, the brand-new coins very rapidly disappeared—because they were hoarded for saving, while the old, bad stuff stayed in circulation because people spent it as fast as they could. Gresham's law was not named as such until the nineteenth century, by which time numerous other examples had emerged to prove how widespread this peculiarity was. It applies to anything that is used for payment. When cigarettes become a currency, as they do among troops in wartime, the good tobacco tends to get smoked while the sketchy stuff gets used as a medium of exchange. In a sense, Gresham's law predates but also prefigures behavioral economics, because it concerns the real-world behavior of people—though, in this case, their behavior is perfectly rational. There is another sense in which Gresham's law reflects the different functions of money—as a store of value, a unit of exchange, and as a medium of exchange. When a coin's store of value begins to unravel, then its information value becomes more important, as a medium of exchange.

UTILITY & RATIONAL ECONOMIC MAN
Page 56

GAME THEORY
Page 94

NEW KINDS OF MONEY
Page 104

DRILL DOWN | In the early twentieth century, the German-born Argentinian trader Silvio Gesell applied Gresham's law by designing a currency that was intended to "rust"—lose its value over time—as traditional money had always done. "Stamp scrip" consisted of certificates that required monthly stamps to be added to them, at the cost of 1 percent each time. People were therefore less inclined to hoard them, but instead would spend them as quickly as possible, thereby keeping the economy moving. This was tested out successfully during the Great Depression in North America and Austria. It was eventually declared illegal by President Franklin Roosevelt in 1933, who feared it would undermine faith in the dollar—but not before the great economist Irving Fisher had adopted the idea in his book *Stamp Scrip*. It remains a powerful idea even now.

FOCUS | *The opposite of Gresham's law is also true. There are certainly times when good money drives out bad—for example, during periods of very high inflation when another currency is available; the bad money has no realistic buying power and disappears from circulation. Examples include the use of US dollars during the Soviet period, or in Zimbabwe during hyperinflation. This is known as Thiers' law.*

GAME THEORY

THE MAIN CONCEPT | The rules of economics are becoming increasingly complicated, so it can sometimes make better sense to view the behavior of people and companies like a game. Game theory was introduced by the mathematician John von Neumann in 1928, and since then as many as 11 game theorists have won the Nobel Prize in Economics. The idea is that intelligent and rational people follow the rules of economic or business games, whether they are zero-sum games—where, in order to win, others have to lose—or non-zero-sum games, which tend to be kinder and more widely beneficial. The problem is that this is another way of formalizing and subjecting to mathematical formulae certain economic behaviors. This is itself subject to a major problem—many people's game strategies may change from one moment to the next on a whim. Then there is the "Nash equilibrium," named for the mathematician John Nash, which sets out a peculiarity: if people know others' strategies, games will often reach an equilibrium that is not actually the most advantageous for anyone, but where no player is motivated to change it. Companies tend to seek strategies that will win them the game whatever their opponents do, for example by moving first or innovating.

DRILL DOWN | This brings us to the famous example of game theory—the Prisoners' Dilemma. Two prisoners held incommunicado for the same offense can either confess or say nothing. If they say nothing, they face the risk that the other prisoner will confess, make a deal with prosecutors, and land them with an even heavier sentence. Although the optimal route would be for both to remain silent, both inevitably confess, hoping in vain that the other one won't. The same kind of effect can be seen in corporate behavior in oligopolies, where businesses keep their prices lower than they would like, for fear that one of their rivals will undercut them. Like so much economic modeling, however, this analysis omits crucial human factors—trust, experience, and knowledge.

FOCUS | *There are people who regard the whole business of game theory as misleading because of the assumption that we are rational, but it has had its uses. President John Kennedy used it to game Khrushchev during the Cuban missile crisis in 1962, for example. But if you really want to know about game theory, watch two movies:* Dr. Strangelove *(1964) about nuclear deterrence, and* A Beautiful Mind *(2001) about the game theorist John Nash.*

THE RISE OF THE QUANTS
Page 44

UTILITY & RATIONAL ECONOMIC MAN
Page 56

EFFICIENT MARKETS
Page 78

INSTITUTIONAL ECONOMICS

THE MAIN CONCEPT | After Thorstein Veblen wrote *The Theory of the Leisure Class* in 1899, institutional economics became one of the dominant economic ideas of the century ahead, certainly in the US. It is—or perhaps more accurately, was—a way of integrating human beings into economics in a Darwinian way. It saw progress as a swirling cascade of changing beliefs, habits, ideas, and human institutions, struggling with the opposing forces of disequilibrium—new innovations and businesses that upset everything else. Institutions evolve just as species do—they survive the cascade or not and are replaced. More recently, the Nobel Prize–winning economist Douglass North looked at the unfashionable question of why some countries thrive and others fail; he came to the conclusion that it has something to do with the strength and reliability of a nation's institutions. North won his prize in 1993, but not before he had developed a version of economic history he called "cliometrics"—looking at hard data through history. Modern institutionalists are focused on real human organizations, as Veblen and his followers were interested not so much in institutions as in technology. A further dispute in this field has been over the role of law in economics, triggered back in 1924 by John Commons's book *The Legal Foundations of Capitalism*.

DRILL DOWN | The problem with institutions, according to the behavioral economists, is that they act as irrationally as people do—and sometimes even more so. Groupthink can make institutions at least as stupid as individuals, and often stupider. Conversely, some of the insights that have emerged in the field of "collective intelligence" imply that groups of people can sometimes manage to go beyond what any of the group's individuals could manage together in terms of performance. So the jury remains out.

FOCUS | *The most challenging idea about institutional economics is the claim that economic rules are mediated through human institutions—which is really what classical economics most stands against. One believes that these laws are to some extent socially constructed; the other believes that they are eternal and universal.*

BEHAVIORAL ECONOMICS
Page 88

THE SHARING ECONOMY
Page 112

PEAK OIL & OIL DEPENDENCY
Page 146

SOCIAL CAPITAL

THE MAIN CONCEPT | The original idea in economics was that prosperity and wealth derive from a combination of land, labor, and capital. But more recently, heterodox economists have argued that this is not enough of an explanation. What about the ability of the planet to sustain life (environmental capital) or the know-how of the people involved (intellectual capital)? And what about their ability to get on with each other, which has became known as "social capital." The major work on the subject was by the communitarian writer Robert Putnam, whose 2000 book *Bowling Alone* revealed that Americans were a great deal less likely to join community groups then than they had been in 1950. The problem with Putnam and the communitarian writers was that their solutions seemed a little sparse, though UK Prime Minister Tony Blair's Third Way philosophy derived from an understanding of social capital. Not all social capital is reckoned to be a good thing. It could, for example, mean a reluctance to embrace outsiders—the kind of social capital that unites right-wing groups—when "bridging capital" assumes that people are brought into the fold. Even so, it is clear that people who trust and support each other, especially when they are poorer, clearly survive the storms of economics better than those who don't.

DRILL DOWN | The issue with social capital is whether it really makes a difference to the economy or not. Putnam's nightmare vision of individual people at the bowling alley, staring sadly up at the TV screens, took place when the US economy was booming. But then again, you might have to question what kind of economic success that was—and you still have to explain why so few outside the elite 1 percent profited so much from the boom. It may be that social capital provides an explanation for why, during the past four decades—when poorer families found themselves more isolated from each other—they also seemed less likely to prosper from the economy that was supposed to be booming around them.

BEHAVIORAL ECONOMICS
Page 88
INSTITUTIONAL ECONOMICS
Page 96
INTELLECTUAL CAPITAL
Page 100

FOCUS | *Putnam gathered his evidence from the success of the Emilia-Romagna region of Italy, with its successful and interconnected networks of small workshops, and where social and business institutions often date back to the twelfth century. Some critics wonder what hope there is for the rest of us, given that our own institutions may often only date back a decade or so.*

INTELLECTUAL CAPITAL

THE MAIN CONCEPT | And what about knowledge, which is also pretty vital to the creation of prosperity? That is where intellectual capital comes in, sometimes known as "knowledge capital," or "human capital." Intellectual capital became important in the 1990s when it was clear that the value of certain companies went a long way beyond the value of their buildings, or even their brand. The term was introduced, perhaps most persuasively, by the financial journalist Thomas Stewart in his 1997 book *Intellectual Capital*, which explored the ability of companies to use their collective brainpower to make a difference by winning an edge over competitors, or exploiting their intellectual property. The difficulty is that intellectual capital is extremely difficult to measure, yet something that companies have to be aware of and to plan for—otherwise it will simply walk out the door and go and work for their competitors. There are other difficulties, too. Some of the know-how—usually the stuff that goes unnoticed by senior managers—really can't be measured at all, including relationships with customers or suppliers, or the people who know, for example, where the screwdrivers are kept in the office. Although these can be crucial when it comes to getting things done, this kind of intellectual capital is next to impossible to communicate on a balance sheet.

BEHAVIORAL ECONOMICS
Page 88
SOCIAL CAPITAL
Page 98
NEW ECONOMIC INDICATORS
Page 102

DRILL DOWN | Human capital does not just apply to companies. A national workforce's skills and willingness to learn provide countries with an obvious economic advantage. If they have a good, broad educational system, which provides young people with creative skills, a nation will thrive, compared with one where the population sits around expecting the same traditional factory job as their forefathers. That is why human capital and its exploitation is assessed as part of a nation's National Intangible Capital (NIC), using a methodology known as ELSS, or Edvinsson-Lin-Ståhle-Ståhle (after its creators). The United States currently sit at the top of NIC rankings, followed by Singapore and then Sweden.

FOCUS | *One of the first signs that a concept like intellectual capital was required came with the dot-com bubble of the late 1990s, when it became clear that a dot-com start-up like AOL had a valuation that was so high that it could take over a well-established bricks-and-mortar business like Time Warner. The result was one of the most dysfunctional mergers of all time.*

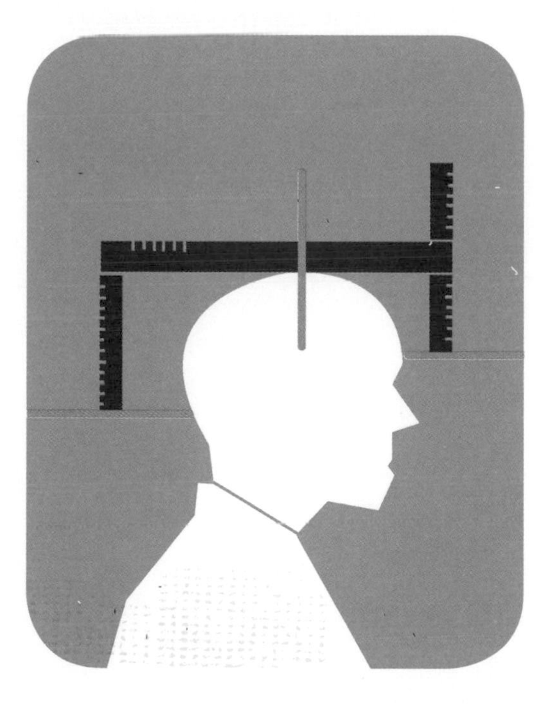

NEW ECONOMIC INDICATORS

THE MAIN CONCEPT | Economic indicators function a bit like traffic signals, speed cameras, and dashboard dials; they advise on the best way ahead, and give feedback to regulate and ensure the safe working of the system. You'll hear talk of growth, interest, unemployment, inflation rates, productivity, savings, and debt levels. The suite of classic economic indicators says a lot about the amount of economic activity taking place, yet not much about its quality. As a result, several other indicators have emerged to measure everything from well-being to the loss of forests in order to give a fuller picture of how successfully an economy is delivering long, happy lives in balance with the environment. Although now heavily criticized, one indicator—growth in GDP—remains profoundly influential. But since the 1970s, several alternatives have been available that adjust growth by also taking account of things ranging from the value of unpaid work and leisure time, to family breakdown, mental health, gaps between rich and poor, and environmental damage. Examples of such indices include the Measure of Economic Welfare, the Index of Sustainable Economic Welfare, and the Measure of Domestic Progress. And to measure human progress, the United Nations developed the composite Human Development Index, including indicators of life expectancy, educational attainment, and income.

UTILITY & RATIONAL ECONOMIC MAN
Page 56

WELL-BEING
Page 106

FEMINIST ECONOMICS
Page 108

DRILL DOWN | The Happy Planet Index is a composite indicator that reveals clear global patterns. Rich countries do badly because they have large ecological footprints. Very low-income countries suffer low life expectancy, so also score poorly. Central America and some parts of South America perform best overall. People there achieve relatively long and satisfied lives with moderate levels of consumption. Within every region the countries that tend to have higher life expectancy and satisfaction, and smaller ecological footprints, are smaller island nations—perhaps because, being smaller, more remote, and therefore vulnerable, they often evolve adaptive, supportive forms of economic and social organization. Also, of course, for them environmental limits are much more obvious and the negative consequences of crossing them much more immediate.

FOCUS | *With so many measures, which should take priority? UK professors Kate Pickett and Richard Wilkinson have reviewed decades of data and concluded that inequality, measured by an indicator called the "Gini coefficient," was the most important. Most major health and social problems are significantly worse in more unequal countries, and people are also less likely to take positive environmental actions when they live in very unequal places.*

NEW KINDS OF MONEY

THE MAIN CONCEPT | Imagine if cash got scarce, or we could reorganize the different functions of money a little differently—a bit less "store of value" or a bit more "medium of exchange" (see page 92). We could—and might need to—then replace mainstream currencies with new kinds of money that might circulate and behave in different ways, and might value things differently. The emergence of bitcoin and similar virtual currencies have shown that this is possible, and the concept has a long history, dating back to the "black money" made from tin and circulated by cities or cathedrals in medieval times. Or, more recently, the various new kinds of money designed to hold their value ("constant currencies"), funnel investment to small businesses ("farm notes"), or provide spending power in struggling communities (the Bristol Pound, Ithaca HOURS, or local exchange trading systems). There is evidence that, despite the trend of some currencies getting bigger and more international, like the euro or US dollar—there is another trend that would see money as more diverse, local, and personal. Certainly when money is scarce, as in wartime, people tend to use whatever is nearest to hand, like cigarettes or food. The advent of computers and electronic wallets on cell phones make electronic versions of money easier to use, but they also open up the possibility of parallel currencies.

INFLATION
Page 64
THE CORE ECONOMY
Page 110
ECO-CURRENCIES
Page 140

DRILL DOWN | New kinds of money have proliferated in times of conventional economic emergency. Stamp scrip (see page 93) circulated widely around the US during the Great Depression, and the Swiss credit system WIR also derived from that period. Local exchange trading systems (LETS) emerged during the early 1990s downturn. The Argentinian Global Clubs de Truque were supporting nearly two million people at their height after Argentina defaulted on its debt in 2000. The latest wave of UK currencies, like the Bristol Pound and the Brixton Pound, both derive from recent downturns after the banking crash of 2007–8.

FOCUS | *Up to a third of world trade was taking place by the 1980s in the form of barter, but assisted by the development of trade dollars or trade pounds, a kind of barter currency that crossed borders and allowed you to barter very different items for what you wanted. Most of this trade was carried out using commercial barter currencies.*

WELL-BEING

THE MAIN CONCEPT | If GDP isn't the whole story of progress, is there a better way to measure human progress? That is the question asked by well-being economists, following in the footsteps of the government of Bhutan, which famously uses a measure they call "gross national contentment." Back in 1995, a group of researchers from the US think-tank Redefining Progress put forward an alternative to GDP in the magazine *Atlantic Monthly*. Their article piled on the evidence against GDP. The *Wall Street Journal* had just worked out that O. J. Simpson's trial in 1995 had cost the equivalent of Grenada's total GDP. Was that progress? Then there were the thousands of liposuction operations taking place every year in the US, pumping thousands of dollars into the GDP figures. The proposal by Herman Daly, John Cobb, and Redefining Progress was known as the Index of Sustainable Economic Welfare (ISEW). This index was plotted against GDP on a chart, revealing that while GDP had gone up inexorably, sustainable welfare had changed direction in the 1970s and started going down. This suggested that we are suffering from the opposite of wealth—what John Ruskin called "illth." In fact, there is little evidence to link rising income in itself with rising happiness, and a lot of evidence that despite accelerating incomes, the degree of happiness has stayed much the same in Western nations for the past half century or so.

DRILL DOWN | In 2010, UK Prime Minister David Cameron pledged to give greater focus to the achievement of happiness and well-being, following on from the introduction of the Happy Planet Index (HPI) in 2006, developed by the New Economics Foundation. The HPI measures the ability of every nation to use raw materials efficiently to produce years of well-being. The first place to top the index was the island state of Vanuatu. The second was Colombia. There have also been a number of other attempts to measure well-being—as a more permanent state than happiness, which can be a bit flighty. Neither can actually be measured objectively, but researchers have learned from medical measures such as "self-reported pain," and have begun to develop similar measures for well-being.

MEDIEVAL ECONOMICS
Page 22
UTILITY & RATIONAL ECONOMIC MAN
Page 56
NEW ECONOMIC INDICATORS
Page 102

FOCUS | *British labor economist Professor Richard Layard has studied happiness, and has suggested a wealth tax on very rich people because their wealth causes measurable unhappiness in other people. There is some evidence that "status" goods, luxury items, and designer logos cause unhappiness in people who can't afford them. They certainly cause envy.*

FEMINIST ECONOMICS

THE MAIN CONCEPT | "Five clerks, all of them women with substantial experience and know-how, assisted importantly with this work." So read a note below the list of men who contributed to the critical work on national accounting by Keynesian economist Simon Kuznets (whose Kuznets curve later assumed a link between the improvement of women's lives and high GDP). But why were they not named alongside the men, asked Marilyn Waring in *If Women Counted* (1988). Her contention was that economic measurements discount women, just as they discount nature, housework, religious work, and all the other activities that build national life but are not measured by economists. Waring presented the example of trees, which have a value in national accounts when they are felled and turned into toothpicks, but not when they are alive. Yet are they not part of our national wealth, just as women are? Feminist economists claim that conventional economic measures—derived from assumptions based on a white, male, and upper-middle-class perspective—are blind to many of the key elements of a broader "wealth." For the same reason, they provide a critique of economic history, looking at rejected ideas and concepts, emphasizing the unmeasured importance of "women's work," and de-emphasizing the traditional focus on competition.

DRILL DOWN | Marilyn Waring says that economists traditionally make the following unjustified assumptions about women:

- All women are married, or if not yet, they will be and all women will have children.
- All women are economically dependent on a male relative.
- All women are (and should be) housewives due to their reproductive capacities.
- Women are unproductive in the industrial workforce.
- Women are irrational, unfit economic agents, and cannot be trusted to make the right economic decisions.

KEYNESIAN ECONOMICS
Page 36
NEW ECONOMIC INDICATORS
Page 102
WELL-BEING
Page 106

FOCUS | *In 1970, the American economist Lisa Leghorn used a survey by Chase Manhattan Bank to work out, using conventional economic measures, what a wife is worth to men. Multiplying these factors by the number of housewives in the country, she ended with a figure that was about half of US GDP at the time, and about twice annual US government spending.*

THE CORE ECONOMY

THE MAIN CONCEPT | The term "core economy" was coined by the economist Neva Goodwin to explain that element of the way we live that underpins the rest of it—family and community, the structures that educate and socialize children, support old people, keep an eye out on the street, and all those other things that traditional economics takes for granted. The core economy provides a hidden subsidy to business, making sure that children know how to eat or that criminals get caught, but where, generally speaking, money does not circulate. Critics say the term relates to sociology rather than economics, yet it certainly has economic implications. The author of *Future Shock* (1970), Alvin Toffler, used to ask American businesses what it would cost them if none of their executives had ever been toilet-trained. The idea builds on those of other academics who are on the fringes of economics yet have made important economic insights. Examples include the architectural critic Jane Jacobs, whose book *The Death and Life of the Great American Cities* (1961) changed people's attitudes to planning, and the political economist Elinor Ostrom, who developed the concept of "coproduction," which shows how professionals such as doctors need patients, as much as the other way around, to achieve their objectives.

DRILL DOWN | One of those who has developed the core-economy idea has been the civil rights lawyer Edgar Cahn, who developed a community-building money system called "time dollars" ("time banks" in Europe). This acts as a kind of parallel currency, and rewards people for the community effort they put in. Time dollars have been used as a tool for public service reform, rewarding people for visiting older people or acting as community jurors or a range of other activities that are vital for the smooth running of society—and which they can use to buy mutual support for themselves or surplus from the mainstream economy.

FOCUS | *The idea of the core economy derives from a branch of economics dubbed socioeconomics or communitarianism, as exemplified by people like Robert Putnam or Amitai Etzioni, both of whom in different ways have developed the way that human interaction is vital to our economic futures.*

SOCIAL CAPITAL
Page 98

NEW KINDS OF MONEY
Page 104

FEMINIST ECONOMICS
Page 108

THE SHARING ECONOMY

THE MAIN CONCEPT | How you understand the sharing economy depends on your point of view. You might believe in the cooperative spirit and welcome technologies that allow us to share things—whether it is spare rooms (Airbnb) or parking spaces (JustPark). Or you might believe in Joseph Schumpeter's "creative destruction," which can destroy cozy hotel or taxi monopolies and allow you to provide your own alternative, or to choose from a variety of new ones. This may depend on you using new technology to give you the economic power to take on the old order. Whatever you call it, the idea is the same—the main difference between the two attitudes is who owns the technology that makes it possible. If, for example, Uber is disrupted successfully by a new provider who spreads the ownership and benefits more widely, then there will be no contradiction—we are not swapping one identikit monopoly for another. But strictly speaking, if the sharing economy is to mean anything, ownership of the new system needs to be wider. There is an argument that, by itself, sharing platforms like Uber are not so much sharing as simply old-fashioned renting. But by reducing transaction costs, such sharing platforms make it possible for ordinary people to rent out their assets on a much wider scale. The danger is that they do so in an unregulated way, and put whole sectors out of business without actually sharing the benefits very widely.

DRILL DOWN | One of the peculiarities of the sharing economy is that it allows people to work on a more informal basis. This is known as the "gig economy," and it is usually popular with those who freelance in this way—though the rules set by their employers are not usually generous and seem likely to get less so. The danger is that employees may be cast off as independent contractors by big employers without wanting to go freelance, adding to their insecurity and limiting their rewards (especially if they must provide their own tools, vacation pay, and insurance). One survey suggests that up to 40 percent of the US workforce will soon be forced to work this way.

COMPARATIVE ADVANTAGE
Page 68
SOCIAL CAPITAL
Page 98
THE COMMONS
Page 138

FOCUS | *One of the most unexpected elements of the sharing economy is what it has done to banking, where people can be put more directly in touch with those who have savings and are willing to lend them. This is already beginning to happen and, in the future, it may lead to better customer service by banks.*

“There is something fundamentally wrong in treating the Earth as if it were a business in liquidation.”

HERMAN DALY,
STEADY-STATE ECONOMICS (1977)

4

ECONOMICS & THE PLANET

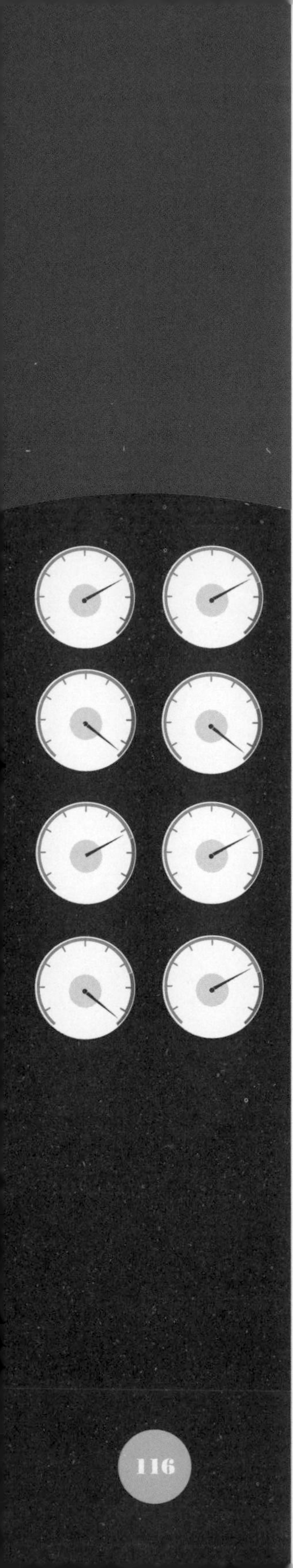

INTRODUCTION

Economics has been described as the practice of keeping house, but on a society-wide scale. At the largest scale of all, our planet, it now faces its biggest challenge. Ideas of sufficiency, and an awareness of the dangers of damaging the environment we depend on, are thousands of years old. Today, with even more pressing urgency, they also include the warnings, now well over 100 years old, that our economic activity and burning of fossil fuels will lead to the Earth's climate heating up, and us losing the oddly convivial conditions that allowed civilization to prosper.

Economics for planetary change

We are finely balanced. The global economy keeps growing, pushing beyond the biosphere's boundaries. But the economic tools, technologies, and human capacity for innovation and change can bring us back from the edge. Many argue that learning to live within our environmental thresholds can bring benefits for our health and well-being, too. This chapter highlights some of the key concepts and approaches.

We start with an entry on green economics (pages 122–23), which introduces the fundamental problem—how much you price the environment into an economic market formula, and to what degree do you bend economics to suit the dictates of the environment? A key example of this comes in the next issue that we cover, one of planetary boundaries (pages 124–25). It was the economist Herman Daly who described the economy as "a subsidiary" of the biosphere. This is not an approach that would have appealed much to the last generation of economists, but heterodox economics is beginning to shift people's attitudes.

An entry on scarcity and the enclosures (pages 126–27) looks more closely at some of these questions. Scarcity is a peculiar concept—absolutely crucial for market economics, but in some ways it does not apply to nature in quite the way we expect. Human attributes of kindness and care are, after all, not scarce at all. Yet they tend to be forgotten for precisely that reason.

Another area where these kinds of argument become apparent is in cost-benefit analysis (pages 128–29), where prices are used to categorize assets, species, places, or some combination of them. It is logical, and sometimes "completely insane," as a former Brazilian environment minister put it, yet it has to be done to develop some real-world solutions.

The circular economy (pages 130–31) suggests one way out of these dilemmas—to reorganize the economy in such a way that its waste products are used increasingly as raw materials. This is now a well-fought and highly topical debate. The entry on the economics of scale (pages 132–33) is a related debate about externalities and the point at which they come to override the benefits of scale in any enterprise, which is a potential challenge to some of the original precepts of the nineteenth-century economics pioneer David Ricardo.

We then explore the human and environmental cost of growth and development (pages 134–35), alongside the issue of ethical consumerism (pages 136–37), which rejects simple profit as the only basis for business, and replaces it with another, more moral dimension.

Exploring the consequences

There then follow a number of entries that cover some of the repercussions of these arguments, starting with the commons (pages 138–39), by which we don't just mean common land, but also all those other areas of economic and human behavior that are governed by cooperation rather than just by competition. Eco-currencies (pages 140–41) looks at how much money ought to be based on the stability of natural assets, as it occasionally has been. We also look at proposals, dating back to the days of the great Victorian reformer Henry George, for land tax (pages 142–43) and eco-taxes (pages 144–45), where we tax resource use or other elements of the economy considered "bad" for whatever reason—and find that there are disadvantages as well as advantages to that approach.

Finally, we look at the arguments around peak oil and oil dependency (pages 146–47), and some of the paradoxes of the so-called "curse of oil" (which is one of them) in a modern economy. We consider whether there will be a point—not far off, perhaps—when oil prices will become so high as to choke off supply suddenly and perhaps disastrously, at least for current assumptions abut the need for fossil fuel.

TIMELINE

11,000 BCE

FARMING

Farming emerges in the so-called Fertile Crescent of Northeast Africa and the Middle East, enabling human groups to generate food surpluses that allow organized settlements and populations to grow. Areas relied on for natural resources grow too, and have done ever since, increasing humanity's environmental impact.

65 CE

SENECA'S LETTERS

Roman man of letters Seneca the Younger coins the idea of "enough": "What difference does it make how much is laid away in a man's safe or in his barns . . . if he is always after what is another's? You ask what is the proper limit to a person's wealth? First, having what is essential, and second, having what is enough."

1760

THE INDUSTRIAL REVOLUTION

Britain begins to shift from a rural, artisanal economy to machine-and factory-based manufacturing, becoming increasingly urban. This evolves into an international phenomenon where transportation, communication, technology, and commodity trade lay the foundations for resource-intensive Western lifestyles.

1859

THE OIL AGE

The modern oil age begins in August when Edwin Drake strikes oil in Titusville, Pennsylvania. His new oil drill starts a rush, signaling the end of dependence on whale oil. It also begins an economic dependence on the fossil fuels responsible for the climatic breakdown of global warming.

ELECTRICITY
Electricity supplies begin modestly with an experiment in the English town of Godalming, where streets are lit with light from hydro power, but it goes on to change how we live. In 1882, Thomas Edison introduces electric light to Manhattan, improving on gas and oil lamps, but leading to higher-energy lifestyles in homes full of appliances.

1885

COMBUSTION ENGINE
As Drake strikes oil in 1859, the first successful gas-fired internal combustion engine is developed in France by Étienne Lenoir. It is developed to run on petroleum and applied in 1885 by Gottlieb Daimler and Karl Benz to a motorcycle and motorcar. The fuel-efficient but polluting diesel engine is developed in 1892 by Rudolf Diesel.

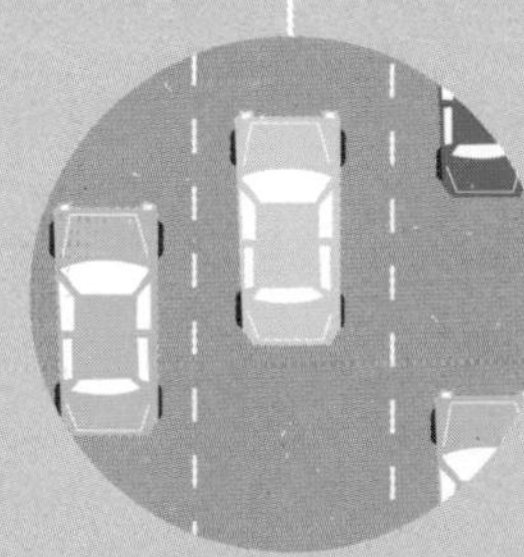

1952

AIR TRAVEL
Modern air travel begins with the de Havilland Comet, the world's first commercial jet airliner. It not only shrinks the world for those who can afford it, and changes eating patterns as previously seasonal, perishable foods become available year round, but also locks in our use of especially harmful fossil fuels.

1960

CONSUMERISM
In 1960 Vance Packard writes *The Waste Makers*, a few years after the term "consumerism" is coined by an executive at the Ford Motor Company as a positive alternative to "capitalism." Packard sees the culture of consumerism, fueled by debt and advertising, as personally harmful, and a damaging pathway to general overconsumption.

BIOGRAPHIES

BARBARA WARD (1914–1981)

The British economist Barbara Mary Ward (later Baroness Jackson) was an important advocate of global economic redistribution in the postcolonial world. She studied economics at Oxford University and was, from 1939, a writer and editor for *The Economist* and later an adviser to the Vatican, the UN, the World Bank, two US presidents, and several UK prime ministers, as well as many heads of state in Asia and Africa. From the 1960s onward, Ward was a key figure in the emergence of environmental awareness and notions of sustainable development. She was associated with the policy that richer, industrialized countries should allocate a certain percentage of their national income to international aid—an idea that became a cornerstone of measures for international assistance and financing development. Ward was the coauthor (with René Dubos) in 1972 of *Only One Earth*, the book that came out of the landmark United Nations Conference on the Human Environment and, shortly before her death in 1979, she published *Progress for a Small Planet*, expressing the need for humanity to cooperate as a "planetary community."

HERMAN DALY (1938–)

Ecological economist Herman Daly, Emeritus Professor at the University of Maryland, witnessed at first hand flaws in mainstream economic development models while working for the World Bank, where he saw that approaches meant to lift populations out of poverty often made matters worse and did great environmental damage, too. He developed the Index of Sustainable Economic Welfare (ISEW) to compensate for socially and environmentally blind measures of economic growth. In his books *Steady-State Economics*, *For the Common Good*, and *Beyond Growth*, Daly built on the work of many half-forgotten or marginalized thinkers like Nicholas Georgescu-Roegen—who argued that economics had to accept the limits imposed by the laws of thermodynamics like every other discipline—and other pioneers like Frederick Soddy, a chemist by training, and systems theorist Richard Buckminster Fuller. Daly's synthesis of their thinking, and that of many others, developed the emerging field of "steady state" and ecological economics that eschews a belief in endless growth and redefines prosperity focused on the quality rather than quantity of economic activity.

DONELLA MEADOWS (1941–2001)

Donella (Dana) Meadows was born in Illinois and trained as a chemist before gaining a PhD in biophysics from Harvard University in 1968. She was a scientist who addressed the problem of the biophysical limits to economic systems. She was also the lead author of the era-defining *The Limits to Growth: A Report for the Club of Rome's Project on the Predicament of Mankind*, published in 1972 by a group of scientists from the Massachusetts Institute of Technology and financed by the Club of Rome. Over nine million copies of the book have been sold in 26 languages. Although criticized at the time, and relying on computer modeling that by today's standards was crude, its projections for the potentially devastating impact from continued economic growth on planetary ecological life-support systems have stood the test of time. In 1992, Meadows co-authored an update, *Beyond the Limits: Confronting Global Collapse, Envisioning a Sustainable Future*. Meadows was a systems thinker who believed that a "small shift in one thing can produce big changes in everything," and she published "twelve leverage points to intervene in a system" in 1997, to enable better decision-making for living within the biosphere's limits. In 1996, Meadows founded the Sustainability Institute (now called the Academy for Systems Change) to carry on the work of applying her systems theory. Its mission was to foster "transitions to sustainable systems at all levels of society, from local to global," and to make her work accessible beyond a community of experts.

JAYATI GHOSH (1955–)

Jayati Ghosh gained her PhD in economics from Cambridge University in the UK and was a visiting professor at Tufts University in the US. She has worked on various official commissions in India, ranging in focus from planning to knowledge and farmers' welfare, and was the principal author of the West Bengal Human Development Report 2004—awarded the UNDP Award for Excellence in Quality of Analysis. A prolific contributor to economic debates, Ghosh is a critic of the impact of conventional finance-driven economic globalization and an advocate of people- and environment-centered economic development models. As an economist who is active in a country with widespread poverty and considered still to be developing, Ghosh's work stands out for its rejection of typical Western expectations of production and consumption. Labeling these destructive and exploitative, Ghosh calls for new approaches that go beyond embracing "cleaner, greener technologies," to thinking creatively about consumption itself.

GREEN ECONOMICS

THE MAIN CONCEPT | Green economics seeks to put nature back into the picture where older schools of thought left it out. Just like people, economies depend utterly on the biosphere and its ecosystems to survive and function. But more conventional approaches to economics tend to treat the things and services that nature provides as "free income," not accounted for in a normal way, or as largely invisible "externalities," existing outside of the economic model. Green economics attempts a more complete understanding of how an economy works, by taking nature and ecosystems into account. Its objective is a harmonious equilibrium between the demands of the human economy and the biosphere's ability to regenerate and sustain life. The approaches within green economics are diverse. Some environmental economists include nature in economic models by putting a price on it. The theory is that natural systems will then be more valued and therefore not dangerously overexploited. But there is no single way of pricing nature or the activities that damage it. And other schools of green economic thinking, such as ecological economics, argue that putting a price on nature makes dangerous overuse more likely; commodifying it enables markets to exploit it. Their preference is to set limits on how much we take from nature, or the waste we dump into it.

PRICE
Page 66
PLANETARY BOUNDARIES
Page 124
COST-BENEFIT ANALYSIS
Page 128

DRILL DOWN | The paradox of environmental economics can be seen in attempts to create a market to control carbon emissions by putting a price on them, as the European Emissions Trading Scheme (ETS) does. In this scheme, permits to emit carbon dioxide trade for a few euros per ton. Yet elsewhere the damage done by a ton of carbon dioxide has been estimated at several hundred dollars. The ETS is also limited in scope—less than global and with a limit to carbon emissions that is not set by the science of avoiding dangerous warming. That means the players in the market will, in theory, be allowed to burn enough carbon to take us past a climate tipping point. So what price would the market put on that extra notional ton of carbon that, once burned, tips the balance and triggers catastrophic and irreversible climate change? This would be like asking, how much is civilization worth?

FOCUS | *One study by the European Commission and the German government estimated that forest loss had an annual price tag of some $2–5 trillion. The great Victorian thinker John Ruskin famously observed that there is "no wealth but life," and many others have noted that all life depends on plants.*

PLANETARY BOUNDARIES

THE MAIN CONCEPT | Herman Daly described the economy as a "subsidiary" of the biosphere. Since the well-being and survival of a subsidiary depends on the health of the parent company, then the fundamental operating space for the economy is the biosphere; its ecological limits set our economic parameters. So what are those limits? In 2009, groundbreaking research set out to define the key "planetary boundaries" that, if crossed, could permanently damage our ecological life-support system: climate change; rate of biodiversity loss; interference with the nitrogen and phosphorus cycle upon which productive agriculture depends; stratospheric ozone depletion; ocean acidification; global freshwater use; change in land use, such as deforestation for farming and urban sprawl; chemical pollution; and "atmospheric aerosol loading" (particulate matter from burning coal, crop waste, and burning forests that ends up as soot, sulfates, and other particles in the atmosphere, and is damaging to both animal health and the climate). The researchers found that three boundaries had already been crossed: climate change, disruption of the nitrogen cycle, and biodiversity loss. We are also at or near four others: ocean acidification, ozone depletion, land-use change, and freshwater use. On the last two (chemical pollution and aerosol loading) they were not yet confident of defining the boundary to say which side of it we might be on.

DRILL DOWN | Setting boundaries is not straightforward. The Earth's systems do not work in isolation—a change to how one functions can influence others. They may react to change in nonlinear ways and suffer domino effects. Overburdening one system can make waves for another, making it less able to carry such a heavy load from human activities as it once did. Put too much carbon dioxide into the atmosphere, increasing the concentration of the gas, for example, and you not only cause climate change, but push ocean acidification too, which in turn has an effect on biodiversity. As the designers of the planetary boundaries pointed out in the science journal *Nature*: "If one boundary is transgressed, then other boundaries are also under serious risk . . . for instance, significant land-use changes in the Amazon could influence water resources as far away as Tibet."

GREEN ECONOMICS
Page 122
THE CIRCULAR ECONOMY
Page 130
ETHICAL CONSUMERISM
Page 136

FOCUS | *As long ago as 1895 a Swedish chemist, Svante Arrhenius, predicted that an economy reliant on burning fossil fuels would create global warming. Without a computer or fancy instruments, he calculated that increasing the concentration of carbon dioxide in the atmosphere by between two and two-and-a-half times would increase temperatures by 38°F (3.4°C). He was remarkably accurate. In the 1990s, scientists on the Intergovernmental Panel on Climate Change predicted a range between 34.7 and 40.1°F (1.5–4.5°C).*

SCARCITY & THE ENCLOSURES

THE MAIN CONCEPT | "Economics" is rooted in the Greek word for "home" and carries the meaning of household management. The next most common description of the discipline (apart from the "dismal science") is that it is the study of the allocation of scarce resources, principally through the mechanism of price. While human wants have no fixed limit, resources typically do; economics is meant to mediate this problem by working out how to allocate resources with the greatest efficiency. But scarcity is relative. Timber is not scarce in Sweden, but it is on Easter Island. Also, there is a difference between "wants"—which can be invented through fashion and marketing—and "needs," the food, clothing, shelter, and human company we need to exist. An economy geared toward the accumulation of private wealth may, through high levels of inequality, artificially create scarcity. Things can be more complicated still. Edgar Cahn, the inventor of "timebanking"—a system whereby people conduct exchanges through the medium of units of their working time—makes the point that certain human resources, such as love and the provision of care, are not scarce at all, but ubiquitous. Despite their importance, in orthodox economics they are hence given little value.

DRILL DOWN | The practice of creating enclosures began in twelfth-century England. The ruling aristocracy took communal land, which was used by the community to graze livestock, and enclosed it with fencing or hedging to remove common rights of use. It accelerated across Europe during the Industrial Revolution and had the effect of making accessible land more scarce to the majority, reducing the self-sufficiency of communities. "Land grabbing" across national borders by states and private corporations is a modern version of this medieval practice. Where land has been held under customary rights by communities, but not enforced with legal documents, foreign investors are able to claim, enclose, and remove rights formerly held in common.

MEDIEVAL ECONOMICS
Page 22

PRICE
Page 66

THE COMMONS
Page 138

FOCUS | *In one decade (2006–16), 491 large-scale land grabs were recorded by the international small-farmer support organization GRAIN. The deals reported were limited to those that had been initiated after 2006, were led by foreign investors, were "active," (i.e., they had not been canceled), were just focused on food production, and were at least 500 hectares (1,230 acres) in size. In total, these deals accounted for 30 million hectares of land across 78 countries.*

COST-BENEFIT ANALYSIS

THE MAIN CONCEPT | Cost-benefit analysis is a tool designed to give a full picture of the likely results of a potential course of action by adding up the likely benefits and subtracting the costs. It is sensitive, however, to what gets included in the calculation, and how prices are given to the elements involved. For example, if you were to assess the proposal to build a supermarket on a town's meadow you would need to come up with a price for the land. You could ask how much a community would be willing to pay to keep the meadow (a value constrained by their means), or how much compensation they might demand for its loss (potentially infinite). London's Heathrow Airport provides a real-world example. In 2009 the UK Secretary of State for Transport approved the building of a third runway, justified in part by analysis that concluded it would bring an economic benefit of £5.5 billion ($6.9 billion). But according to a more comprehensive assessment, which included harm to the local community, and had revised estimates of likely economic growth and a higher price of carbon, the net cost to society outweighed the benefits by at least £5 billion, and up to £7.5 billion.

DRILL DOWN | In 1991, Chief Economist to the World Bank, Lawrence Summers, wrote, "I think the economic logic behind dumping a load of toxic waste in the lowest wage country is impeccable." His logic: as the costs of "health impairing pollution" were determined by the earnings lost as a result of death or illness, if wages in a country were low, the costs would be lower, so it made sense to pollute the poor. Brazil's Secretary of the Environment, José Lutzenburger, replied, "Your reasoning is perfectly logical but totally insane," calling it an example of "unbelievable alienation, reductionist thinking, social ruthlessness, and the arrogant ignorance of many conventional 'economists.'"

FOCUS | *After writing his infamous memo, Lawrence Summers wasn't censured, but went on in 1999 to become the US Treasury Secretary and later President of Harvard University. However, José Lutzenburger, who called for his removal from the World Bank, was fired shortly after writing his letter.*

PRICE
Page 66
PLANETARY BOUNDARIES
Page 124
ETHICAL CONSUMERISM
Page 136

THE CIRCULAR ECONOMY

THE MAIN CONCEPT | The circular economy means a shift from waste to "endless resourcefulness." The mainstream economy is still based on a throughput of resources with waste coming out the other end, with disposability and obsolescence built into products. The circular economy is the opposite, with durable products that are designed for reuse and that retain their value. They should never end up in landfill as waste, nor should they be broken into parts and used for something else. So-called consumables, products with short life spans, should be designed for maximum use and safe reintegration into the environment. The circular economy demands what is termed "one-planet living." Natural resources should only be used at a rate at which the biosphere can regenerate them. A fully circular economy would arrive at an equilibrium in which the volume of resources consumed did not grow. One great benefit of a circular economy is the creation of jobs in the environmental sectors—the International Labour Organization sees the potential for tens of millions of new "green-collar" jobs.

DRILL DOWN | Aspects of a modern circular economy—minimizing waste and maximizing maintenance, repairability, and product longevity—would have been second nature to most people up to the 1960s. But the contemporary version is driving innovation. The "circular supply" approach substitutes nonrenewable resources with renewable equivalents. It employs resource recovery and extends product life. Sharing platforms allow underused assets to be shared, improving utilization and reducing demand. Companies are shifting to providing products as services, rather than "sell and forget." In this model, customers have either a lease or pay-for-use arrangement—in which the produce remains owned and maintained by the provider, who is also responsible for its ultimate end-of-life management.

THE SHARING ECONOMY
Page 112
PLANETARY BOUNDARIES
Page 124
ETHICAL CONSUMERISM
Page 136

FOCUS | *Between 1980 and 2000, the human population's total use of resources rose dramatically, up by 2.5 percent per year from 35 billion tons. But for every dollar of output, we used fewer resources, suggesting better efficiency and "decoupling." But from 2000 things reversed—resource use rose faster than growth (a kind of "recoupling"), meaning we became more wasteful.*

THE ECONOMICS OF SCALE

THE MAIN CONCEPT | Scale matters. A firework is fun, a bomb is not. How big should things get in the economy? Early economists like David Ricardo and J. S. Mill believed economies would grow to a certain size and then level off. But today, the default assumption, whether it's a company or a whole economy, is that growth is good. Yet many also argue that appropriateness of scale is one of the most important issues for economics to work as if people and the planet mattered. For example, if the economy outgrows its supporting biosphere, there is a problem. Or, a single currency over a very large, diverse area can prove problematic—the different economic circumstances found across the European Union, for example, need different interest rates, which the euro (used in large parts of Europe) doesn't allow. Some ecological economists suggest that economies should be organized according to their biological regions. E. F. Schumacher argued in favor of the principle of "subsidiarity"—organizing things at the lowest or smallest practical level, to prevent them becoming inefficient, inhuman, or impressive. One reason why companies become big is the belief in the economies of scale that result from specialization and increasing thesize of operation. A classic example was when Henry Ford introduced his moving assembly line in 1913, hugely raising productivity. But the opposite—diseconomies of scale—are now widely recognized.

DRILL DOWN | Karl Marx criticized the prevailing culture's belief in economies of scale in agriculture, arguing that smaller farms could achieve the same economies by associating together for joint tasks like marketing. Before and after Marx, radicals like William Cobbett and economists like Amartya Sen noticed the phenomenon of diseconomies of scale on farms: both argued that poor land and small units tend to produce more efficiently than large units on good land. Why? Because of the attention to detail that is possible in the small units.

FOCUS | *The brewing billionaire Freddie Heineken argued that Europe would be better managed as 50 small nations than half the number of larger ones. He also proposed splitting England into seven. Why? Because it would avoid the diseconomies of scale.*

PRODUCTIVITY
Page 58

MONOPOLIES
Page 74

GROWTH & DEVELOPMENT
Page 134

GROWTH & DEVELOPMENT

THE MAIN CONCEPT | It was once generally believed that economic growth was a panacea for human progress and development. And, in very poor countries, an increase in wealth does improve people's chances. But the picture is more complicated. In its landmark 1996 Human Development Report, the United Nations Development Programme identified five types of negative economic growth seen in both capitalist or socialist societies. Both, it said, had a tendency to "sacrifice" people on the "altar of increased accumulation." "Jobless growth" is when an economy gets bigger, without creating more jobs, experienced in countries from India to Egypt and Ghana. "Voiceless growth" is when an economic strategy suppresses civil rights, union membership, and democracy, as has been seen in parts of East Asia and elsewhere. "Ruthless growth" is characterized by high or rising inequality, and has been the experience of the UK and the US, and countries ranging from India to South Africa, with Brazil famously unequal. "Rootless growth" describes the culturally destructive effects of economic globalization, such as the erosion of diversity and the cloning impacts of chains like McDonalds and Starbucks. "Futureless growth" is when economic expansion rides on unsustainable consumption of finite resources.

DRILL DOWN | Problems arise when growth becomes an end in itself in an economic plan, rather than attempting to achieve progress in the things that growth is meant to deliver, such as better health, literacy, and life satisfaction. Bodies like the United Nations have begun compiling more nuanced pictures of the progress of nations with measures like UNDP's Human Development Index (HDI). This combines measures of life expectancy, educational attainment, and income to give a fuller picture of social and economic development. Its 2011 report noted rising inequality in much of the world, and carbon emissions were strongly linked to rising income while progress in concerns such as health and education was not.

GLOBALIZATION
Page 40
NEW ECONOMIC INDICATORS
Page 102
WELL-BEING
Page 106

FOCUS | *If resources were available to answer all the current unmet need for family planning up to the year 2050, it would lower the world's carbon emissions by 17 percent. Costa Rica and the Russian Federation have been ranked almost identically with the HDI, yet in terms of income, Costa Rica is far poorer. The small island state of Vanuatu (see also page 107) achieves the same level of human development as mighty South Africa.*

ETHICAL CONSUMERISM

THE MAIN CONCEPT | Ethical consumerism is the idea that we can shop our way to a better world. Whether you are concerned about the behavior of banks or the rights of animals or factory workers, or whether you want the most energy-efficient appliance or products made of environmentally friendly recycled materials, the theory is that you can vote with your consumer power to make things better. The inverse of making positive purchase choices, but still part of ethical consumerism, is to boycott products considered to be unethical. In Britain, in 1791, antislavery campaigners led a boycott of sugar produced under conditions of slavery. Hundreds of thousands were estimated to have joined the boycott, with sales falling by a third to a half. "Ethical" sugar was brought onto the market from producers who did not practice slavery—advertised as sugar "not made by slaves." In the 1980s there was a wave of "green consumerism," and similar marketing techniques have been used since to encourage the purchase of goods made locally, grown organically, or traded fairly. The fashion industry has also begun experimenting with more ethical and sustainable ways of doing things. Ethical consumerism suggests that major matters can be tackled without changing the underlying economic model.

DRILL DOWN | Ethical consumerism struggles to get a sufficient share of the market to bring about meaningful change. According to the Organic Trade Association, the US organic market represents just 5.5 percent of food sold in retail outlets. Communicating the ethical credentials of a product to consumers via labeling schemes is also problematic; as soon as more than one scheme becomes available, confusion and lack of consumer confidence can result. The consumer group Which? discovered that confusion over recycling symbols was "rife." Nearly half of people misunderstood a common symbol to mean an item was recyclable, when it actually meant that the producer supported a recycling scheme.

FOCUS | *Your memory plays tricks on you when you try to shop ethically, according to studies published in the* Journal of Consumer Research. *Consumers are worse at remembering bad ethical information about a product (for example, if child labor was involved in its making, or it was made in a polluting manner), than they are at remembering good ethical information (such as if it was carbon neutral, fairly traded, or made with recycled materials).*

UTILITY & RATIONAL ECONOMIC MAN
Page 56
GREEN ECONOMICS
Page 122
THE CIRCULAR ECONOMY
Page 130

THE COMMONS

THE MAIN CONCEPT | Amid the bustle of a market economy, you might be surprised by how much you are surrounded by, and utterly dependent on, a completely different system. It's one that you own, and have as much right to as everyone else, and it is called "the commons." You couldn't live without it, nor could the economy function, yet it often gets taken for granted. The commons are those resources that belong to, or affect, the whole community, and include the air you breathe and the water you drink. The commons embraces most of the streets you may walk or drive down, the parks where you go to relax, and your culture's oldest stories, dances, and musical traditions. But it's more than that, too. It's open-source software, pictures and documents published under the Creative Commons license, and a huge range of public services, from weather forecasting to the fire service.
In his famous essay "The Tragedy of the Commons" (1968), Garret Hardin argued that the commons was a fatally flawed way to manage resources, as unrestrained self-interested motivations for short-term gain would lead to overuse and exhaustion. Issues like climate change have brought about a renewed interest in the commons and the practice of "commoning."

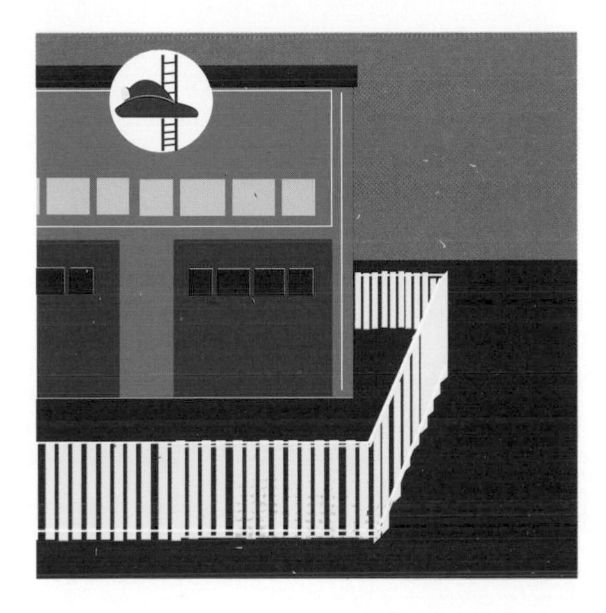

DRILL DOWN | Seemingly in contradiction to Hardin's argument, communal management of shared resources has in fact proven resilient and successful throughout history in the face of environmental extremes, providing more equal access to daily needs than competitive, individualistic market systems based on private property. But Hardin wasn't so much arguing against the commons, but in favor of the need for rules to govern them, writing, "When men mutually agreed to pass laws against robbing, mankind became more free, not less so." Management of the commons, however, becomes difficult at large scales, as with the Earth's climate, where no coherent community or system of government exists.

FOCUS | *The opening verse of a seventeenth-century English folk song about tensions surrounding the commons:*
The law locks up the man or woman
Who steals the goose from off the common
But leaves the greater villain loose
Who steals the common from off the goose.

THE CORE ECONOMY
Page 110

PLANETARY BOUNDARIES
Page 124

SCARCITY & THE ENCLOSURES
Page 126

ECO-CURRENCIES

THE MAIN CONCEPT | Over lunch in Escondido, California, in 1972, the pioneering green economist Ralph Borsodi read that the Federal Reserve was devaluing the dollar. In a rage, he designed what he called an "honest money system." It was supposed to counteract the inflation that follows when money is based on nothing but debt. He called it the "constant" and he based the value on a basket of minerals and agricultural produce arbitraged while it was on the high seas by a group of student volunteers operating out of his home in Exeter, New Hampshire. The constant echoed an idea by Keynes, whose vetoed plan for an economic system after World War II included an underpinning international currency based on commodities like wheat or oil. This kind of stability was urgent during the postwar famine years in Europe: the grand old man of investment banking Benjamin Graham proposed a global currency based on the value of food kept in stores around the world. Most recently, there has been the plan by one of the original designers of the euro, Bernard Lietaer, for the "terra"—a world currency based on a basket of commodities (anything from copper to sugar) that would keep all other currencies stable.

DRILL DOWN | The green economist Richard Douthwaite proposed four currencies inside a single nation. First, an international currency for trading between nations, keeping the global economy within the trading capacity of the planet. Second, a national-exchange currency for trading inside that nation, issued interest-free by the central bank to encourage commercial activity. Third, user-controlled local currencies, to underpin different aspects of local life. And fourth a store-of-value currency, for saving—for houses and other capital assets, linking individual savings to the prosperity of the nation. One of the most widely debated eco-currencies has been kilowatt hours, generated by renewable energy, which has pretty much the same value anywhere.

FOCUS | *The constant was a success. The University of New Hampshire Press was soon printing 275,000 constants in different denominations up to 100. The local council in Exeter, New Hampshire, even started accepting them as payment for parking fines. Bemused locals tried to understand why their constants were worth $2 one week, but $2.05 a week or so later.*

GRESHAM'S LAW
Page 92
NEW KINDS OF MONEY
Page 104
PLANETARY BOUNDARIES
Page 124

LAND TAX

THE MAIN CONCEPT | Seemingly a celebration of ruthless capitalist accumulation, few realize the origins of the game of Monopoly were an attempt to expose the evils of land speculation. The American Elizabeth Magie Phillips invented the precursor to the game (called The Landlord's Game) in 1903 and gave its streets names like Beggarman's Court and Easy Street. George Street was a nod to US economist and journalist Henry George, who reported the injustices of landlordism. He developed what became known as the "single tax" on land as a remedy to the resulting extreme inequalities. Today, with the cost of housing and property speculation back at the top of the political agenda (house prices in New York State, for example, have increased seven times over since 1980), debate around land taxes has returned. The reason is not the cost of the bricks and mortar but the land beneath them. People without properties already are priced out, and inequality increases between both regions and generations. Land on which planning permission for a housing development is granted accrues a windfall. A hectare of farmland worth £20k without planning consent can rise in price toward £2m if a local authority zones the land for housing. But without a land tax, the benefits are reaped by the private landowner, not the public.

MONOPOLIES
Page 74
SCARCITY & THE ENCLOSURES
Page 126
THE COMMONS
Page 138

DRILL DOWN | The windfall incomes from rising house and land prices have been fed significantly by a financialized, speculative market model that has shifted away from providing social housing, and toward a private market that Henry George would have recognized. In 2018, the British Labour Party proposed a form of land tax (so-called "planning gain") to tackle this unearned income. The proposal was that land intended for the building of new social housing could be bought at preplanning consent prices. This operates, in effect, as a 100 percent windfall tax. This would reduce the cost of building 100,000 such homes per year by an estimated £10 billion, and lower the cost of building a two-bedroom apartment in a Southeast English commuter town by around £80,000. Other responses to the unaffordability of land driving high housing costs have included the formation of unions for renters.

FOCUS | *The original game of Monopoly featured a poorhouse, and if you trespassed on Lord Blueblood's Estate you were sent to prison. You could collect money to buy your basic goods on squares marked "absolute necessity." The game lost its original purpose when a sharp salesman stole the idea for the game from the Quakers during the Great Depression and sold it to a games manufacturer.*

ECO-TAXES

THE MAIN CONCEPT | It is often said that we should tax more of what we want less of, and less of what we want more of. From there, it's a small step to the case for taxing environmentally damaging activities. Taxes have been given a bad name. The accountancy industry facilitates their minimization. Conservative politicians pledge to reduce them. But taxes are the price we pay for civilization. They pay for schools and hospitals, infrastructure, and the law, and the way they are organized can encourage or discourage different activities—tax "breaks" might stimulate renewable energy, say, while higher carbon prices are intended to encourage a move away from the use of fossil fuels that worsen climate upheaval. The US, for example, pays the most in fossil fuel subsidies of all the G7 nations—estimated to be around $26 billion a year. Meanwhile, the UK government says that an eco-tax should be explicitly linked to official environmental objectives, have as its primary objective to encourage environmentally positive behavior, and be set so that the more polluting the behavior, the greater the tax levied. Examples of eco-taxes include the Climate Change Levy, Landfill Tax, and taxes on single-use plastics. Some argue that the income raised should be used to support environmental initiatives, a concept known as "hypothecation," where taxes are linked to spending.

DRILL DOWN | The benefits of eco-taxes can be canceled out if, simultaneously, the tax system is being used to support environmentally damaging industries. This is the case in the UK, where tax breaks have been given to the North Sea oil and gas industry at the same time as support for renewable energy has been cut. Air pollution is linked with one in every eight deaths in the UK. The UK's annual health bill related to air pollution—mostly derived from the burning of oil and gas fuel products—was estimated at £20 billion, or more than two decades' worth of current tax income from the oil and gas sector. In one year, 2015–16, the UK government gave more in subsidies and tax breaks to the North Sea oil and gas industry than it received in tax income from them—going £24 million into the red.

GREEN ECONOMICS
Page 122
PLANETARY BOUNDARIES
Page 124
THE CIRCULAR ECONOMY
Page 130

FOCUS | *Denmark has the highest environmentally related tax revenue in the world. A carbon dioxide tax reduced carbon emissions by around 15 percent per person between 1990 and 2005. Their waste tax has also led to a large decrease in landfill waste, giving hope to countries looking to employ a similar scheme.*

PEAK OIL & OIL DEPENDENCY

THE MAIN CONCEPT | In an age of rapidly rising clean, green renewable energy, the oil and gas industry may seem like it belongs to a bygone age. The smoke and emissions from oil-powered engines should be giving way to electricity from the wind and sun. In fact our dependence on fossil fuels is still huge, with consumption still growing. Not only does that create problems like climate change and deaths from air pollution, it is a big economic problem, too. Our economy is so dependent on fossil fuels—oil especially—for transportation, farming, manufacturing, and more, that any sudden change in price or availability threatens an instant economic shock. It's happened before, such as around 2008 when prices rocketed. Estimates vary about when, but the exhaustion of oil supplies is a geological inevitability. They were a once-in-a-planetary-eon inheritance from the rotting vegetation of the Carboniferous Period, 300 million years ago, much of which we've burned through in just a couple of centuries, and mostly in a few decades. We are now long past the point of peak discoveries of new oil resources, and when the lines on the graph for demand and supply head in opposite directions, an economic shock becomes inevitable.

DRILL DOWN | Geologist Colin Campbell estimated that the boost to productivity given by our oil-based energy system is equivalent to a workforce of 22 billion carbon slaves. Fossil fuels supply 82 percent of global energy, and the amount we use has more than doubled since 1971. Despite the risks of dependence on oil, demand is predicted to grow until at least 2040, but research suggests oil supply will peak before 2030—and possibly 2020. Charles Hall and Kent Klitgaard argue that if oil goes through the path of growth, plateau, and decline ("peak oil"), with a financial market built on the assumption of unfettered growth, then "something has to give."

FOCUS | *Discovery of new global oil sources peaked as long ago as the 1960s. American geologist M. King Hubbert, who worked for Shell Oil, noticed that the curves for oil depletion were quite predictable and estimated in 1956 that production from the lower 48 US states would peak between 1965 and 1970. Production actually peaked between 1970 and 1971.*

DEMAND & SUPPLY
Page 62
PLANETARY BOUNDARIES
Page 124
ECO-TAXES
Page 144

GLOSSARY

APR—annual percentage rate, usually quoted as the annual charge on a loan.

AUSTRIAN SCHOOL—an economic school of thought that arose with a group of anti-Nazi, free-market economists and philosophers who led the postwar movement back to markets.

BARTER—exchanging goods or services without the use of money.

BOND—effectively an IOU, commonly issued by governments and large corporations in order to raise funds.

BOOKKEEPING—accounting for the profitability of a business.

BRETTON WOODS CONFERENCE—or United Nations Monetary and Financial Conference. The 1944 conference held outside Washington, D.C. that set out the financial architecture for the world.

BUBBLE—when the prices for assets rise, through human intervention, way beyond what logic might suggest.

CAPITAL—money or assets used to create wealth; traditionally the third pillar, along with land and labor.

CARBON SLAVE—or energy slave. The amount of energy required to construct or operate an element of nonhuman infrastructure, measured in terms of the productivity of a single person.

CHICAGO SCHOOL—a school of economic thought that originated out of the University of Chicago—the original home of economic liberalism, but now seen as the keeper of the flame of economic orthodoxy.

COMMONS—land, air, and water, provided for free by nature or tradition.

COMMUNITARIANISM—an economic approach that emphasizes the importance of morality and social capital.

COMPARATIVE ADVANTAGE—a theory first proposed by David Ricardo in the nineteenth century, identifying the element in trade that a city or nation is best at.

CORN LAWS—repealed in 1846 in the UK, before which they kept the price of staple agricultural goods unnaturally high in an attempt to support landowners.

CYCLES—various theories suggest that economics has seasonal fluctuations spanning periods of growth and recession. A cycle can span a year, a decade, or sometimes longer.

DARWINISM—economics that emphasizes the survival of the fittest, after Charles Darwin's theory of biological evolution.

ENCLOSURES—a process starting in sixteenth-century England whereby common land was parceled up and then sold.

FEUDAL—the structure of medieval society, deferential and owing allegiance to the local aristocracy.

FINANCIALIZATION—the word coined for the modern process whereby all assets become financial ones.

FREE TRADE—the right to do business with whom you want.

GAME THEORY—introduced by the mathematician John von Neumann, the study of strategic decision-making in scenarios made up of two or more rational competing participants.

GDP (gross domestic product)—the value of the total business (goods produced and services provided) carried out over a year in a given nation.

GIG ECONOMY—a labor market characterized by work that is offered on a temporary or freelance basis.

GREAT DEPRESSION—the global economic collapse that followed the Wall Street Crash of 1929.

GROWTH—this normally refers to the growth in GDP.

HEDGE FUND—a pooled capital fund, usually based offshore in its legal position, which uses investors' money to speculate in new ways. (Hedging involves offsetting risk—as in "hedging your bets.")

HETERODOX—accepting truths from multiple sources, traditions, and experts.

HOMO ECONOMICUS—the reductionist idea that a "rational economic person" exists in the real world.

HYPOTHECATION—the pledging of an asset to secure a loan, or assigning tax revenue to a particular purpose.

IMF (International Monetary Fund)—a lender of last resort for nation-states. Created in 1945, and governed and accountable to 189 different countries.

INDICATORS—numerical measures of nonmonetary success.

INFLATION—the process whereby prices rise because there is too much money chasing too few goods.

INVISIBLE HAND—or hidden hand. Adam Smith's idea, introduced in his *Wealth of Nations*, that the market is moved by the combined needs and wants of people.

LIABILITY—the opposite of an asset: a person's or company's liability includes their obligations to pay someone or to provide them with goods or services.

LOAN SHARKS—shadowy door-to-door purveyors of money at high rates of interest.

MARKETS—one of the many places or systems where people exchange goods or services.

MARXISM—the social and political theories of Karl Marx.

MONETARY—of money, usually its quantity.

MONOPOLY—a market that is dominated by just one firm producing products with no close rival.

OLIGOPOLY—a market that is dominated by a small number of large firms.

OECD (Organization for Economic Cooperation and Development)—an intergovernmental think tank with 36 member countries, founded in 1961 to promote economic growth and world trade.

PRECARIAT—a term combining "precarious" with "proletariat," coined by the British economic writer Guy Standing to describe the growing number of people who lead precarious day-to-day economic lives.

PRICE—the amount of money set by the market for goods or services.

REDUCTIONISM—any idea that reduces the complexity and depth of the world to narrow and inaccurate economic measures.

SELF-EMPLOYED—people who employ themselves rather than work for a company or other employer.

SECURITY—a tradable financial asset.

SEIGNIORAGE—the profit that governments can make when putting cash into circulation because the cost of producing the currency is less than the value of that currency. The same applies to anyone else who creates money. These are controversial issues but, if banks create money in the form of loans—and that seems to be the case—then they will also earn seigniorage.

SOCIAL CAPITAL—the relationships or networks that exist between the various members of a social group.

STAGFLATION—combining "stagnation" and "inflation," a situation that is characterized by slow growth and high inflation and unemployment. Stagflation hit the world in the 1970s.

STIMULI—actions that are taken by governments in order to stimulate sectors of the economy.

SUBSIDIARY—normally a company that is wholly owned by a larger one.

SUSTAINABLE—able to continue without outside intervention, usually in relation to the planetary environment.

TECHNOCRACY—those wedded to a mechanical conception of the world and how it works.

THIRD WAY—a brand of political centrism, associated mainly with the UK Prime Minister Tony Blair.

UNDP (United Nations Development Programme)—the United Nations' global development network, founded in 1965. The UNDP operates across more than 170 countries to help eradicate poverty and reduce inequalities.

UTILITARIANISM—a philosophy that normally judges the most ethical act to be the one that achieves the greatest good, or well-being, for the greatest number of people.

WORLD BANK—a development bank set up alongside the International Monetary Fund (IMF) by the Bretton Woods Conference of 1944. The World Bank was established to provide low-interest loans to developing countries.

ZERO-SUM GAME—in game theory, a situation whereby the gains that are made by the winners are exactly equal to the losses made by the losers.

FURTHER READING

Bishop, Matthew. *Economics: An A–Z Guide*. London: Profile Books, 2003.

Blinder, Alan. *After the Music Stopped.* London: Penguin, 2013.

Blustein, Paul. *The Chastening*. New York: Little, Brown, 2001.

Bourguignon, François. *The Globalization of Inequality*. Princeton: Princeton University Press, 2016.

Boyle, David (ed.). *The Money Changers: Currency Reform from Aristotle to e-cash.* London: Earthscan, 2002.

Broadberry, Stephen, et al. *British Economic Growth, 1270–1870.* Cambridge, UK: Cambridge University Press, 2015.

Cable, Vince. *After the Storm.* London: Atlantic, 2016.

Cahn, Edgar. *No More Throwaway People: The Co-Production Imperative.* Washington, D.C.: Essential Books, 2000.

Chang, Ha Joon. *Bad Samaritans: The Myth of Free Trade.* New York: Bloomsbury, 2010.

Clark, Gregory. *A Farewell to Alms: A Brief Economic History of the World.* Princeton: Princeton University Press, 2007.

Cobb, Clifford, et al. "If the GDP is Up, Why is America Down?" *Atlantic Monthly*, October 1995.

Daly, Herman, "From Adjustment to Sustainable Development: The Obstacle of Free Trade." In Ralph Nader (ed.), *The Case Against Free Trade: GATT, NAFTA, and the Globalization of Corporate Power*. Berkeley, California: North Atlantic Books, 1993.

Daly, Herman. *Beyond Growth: The Economics of Sustainable Development*. Boston, Massachusetts: Beacon Press, 1997.

Daly, Herman. *Steady-State Economics*. Washington, D.C.: Island Press, 1991.

Daly, Herman, and John Cobb. *For the Common Good: Redirecting the Economy Toward Community, the Environment, and a Sustainable Future*. Boston, Massachusetts: Beacon Press, 1989.

Diamond, Jared. *Guns, Germs, and Steel.* New York: Vintage, 1997.

Dincecco, Mark. *Political Transformations and Public Finances: Europe, 1650–1913.* Cambridge: Cambridge University Press, 2011.

Dixit, Avinash, and Barry Nalebuff. *Thinking Strategically: The Competitive Edge in Business, Politics, and Every Day Life.* New York: Norton, 1991.

Douthwaite, Richard. *Short Circuit: Strengthening Local Economies for Security in an Unstable World.* Totnes, UK: Green Books, 1996.

Eichengreen, Barry. *Globalizing Capital: A History of the International Monetary System,* 2nd ed. Oxford: Oxford University Press, 2008.

Eichengreen, Barry. *Hall of Mirrors.* Oxford: Oxford University Press, 2016.

Elgin, Duane. *Voluntary Simplicity.* New York: William Morrow, 1993.

Findlay, Ronald, and Kevin H. O'Rourke. *Power and Plenty: Trade, War, and the World Economy in the Second Millennium.* Princeton: Princeton University Press, 2007.

Frank, Andre Gunder. *ReORIENT: The Silver Age in Asia and the World Economy.* Berkeley, California: University of California Press, 1998.

Friedman, Thomas L. *The Lexus and the Olive Tree.* London: HarperCollins, 1999.

Gordon, Robert. *The Rise and Fall of American Growth.* Princeton: Princeton University Press, 2016.

Haldane, Andrew, and Robert May. "Systemic Risk in Banking Ecosystems." *Nature* no. 469, January 2011.

Hall, Charles, and Kent Klitgaard. *Energy and the Wealth of Nations: Understanding the Biophysical Economy.* New York: Springer, 2011.

Harford, Tim. *The Undercover Economist.* Oxford: Oxford University Press, 2005.

Hayek, Friedrich. *The Road to Serfdom.* London: Routledge Classics, 2001.

Irwin, Douglas, *Against the Tide: An Intellectual History of Free Trade.* Princeton: Princeton University Press, 1996.

Jackson, Tim. *Prosperity Without Growth.* London: Routledge, 2016.

Jacobs, Jane. *Cities and the Wealth of Nations.* New York: Random House, 1986.

Jacobs, Jane. *The Economy of Cities.* New York: Vintage, 1970.

Kay, John. *The Truth about Markets.* London: Penguin, 2003.

Keynes, John Maynard. "National Self-Sufficiency." *The Yale Review*, vol. 22, no. 4, June 1933.

King, Mervyn. *The End of Alchemy: Money, Banking and the Future of the Global Economy.* London: Little, Brown, 2016.

Krugman, Paul. *The Return of Depression Economics*. London: Allen Lane, 2008.

Levitt, Steven, and Stephen Dubner. *Freakonomics: A Rogue Economist Explores the Hidden Side of Everything*. London: HarperCollins, 2005.

Lietaer, Bernard. *The Future of Money*. London: Random Century, 2000.

Maddison, Angus. *The World Economy: Historical Statistics*. Paris: Organization for Economic Cooperation and Development, 2003.

Meadows, Donella, Jorgen Randers, and Dennis Meadows. *The Limits to Growth*. London: Earthscan, 2005.

Mishan, E. J. *The Costs of Economic Growth*. London: Staples Press, 1967.

Mlodinow, Leonard. *The Drunkard's Walk: How Randomness Rules Our Lives*. New York: Pantheon, 2008.

Nye, John. *War, Wine, and Taxes*. Princeton: Princeton University Press, 2007.

O'Rourke, Kevin, and Jeffrey Williamson. *Globalization and History*. Boston, Massachusetts: MIT Press, 1999.

Pearce, David, et al. *Blueprint for a Green Economy*. London: Earthscan, 1989.

Piketty, Thomas. *Capital in the Twenty-First Century*. Cambridge, Massachusetts: Harvard University Press, 2013.

Porritt, Jonathon. *Capitalism as if the World Mattered*. London: Earthscan, 2007.

Raworth, Kate. *Doughnut Economics: Seven Ways to Think Like a 21st-Century Economist*. London: Random House, 2017.

Rosenberg, Nathan, and L. E. Birdzell, Jr. *How the West Grew Rich*. New York: Tauris, 1996.

Schumacher, E. F. *Small is Beautiful: Economics as if People Mattered*. London: Antony Blond, 1973.

Scott Cato, Molly. *Market, Schmarket*. Cheltenham, UK: New Clarion Press, 2006.

Simms, Andrew. *Cancel the Apocalypse*. London: Little, Brown, 2013.

Simms, Andrew and David Boyle. *The New Economics: A Bigger Picture*. London: Earthscan, 2009.

Skidelsky, Robert. *John Maynard Keynes Vol 2: The Economist as Saviour*. London: Picador, 1992.

Smith, Adam. *An Inquiry into the Nature and Causes of the Wealth of Nations.* In R. H. Campbell and A. S. Skinner (eds.), *Glasgow Edition of the Works and Correspondence of Adam Smith* vol. 2. Oxford: Oxford University Press, 1976.

Stern, Nicholas. *The Economics of Climate Change.* London: HM Treasury, 2006.

Stiglitz, Joseph. *Globalization and its Discontents.* New York: Norton, 2002.

Stiglitz, Joseph and Linda Bilmes. *The Three Trillion Dollar War.* New York: Norton, 2008.

Titmuss, Richard. *The Gift Relationship: From Human Blood to Social Policy.* London: New Press, 1970.

Turner, Adair. *Between Debt and the Devil.* Princeton: Princeton University Press, 2016.

Waring, Marilyn. *If Women Counted: A New Feminist Economics.* London: Macmillan, 1988.

Wilkinson, Richard, and Kate Pickett. *The Spirit Level.* London: Penguin, 2011.

INDEX

ABOUT THE AUTHORS

David Boyle is a cofounder of the think tank New Weather Institute, a fellow of the New Economics Foundation, and has been at the heart of the effort to develop coproduction and introduce time banks to Britain as a critical element of public service reform. In 2012–13 he was the government's independent reviewer on the Barriers to Choice Review, assessing public demand for choice in public services. David is the author of a number of books about social change and the future. *Authenticity: Brands, Fakes, Spin and the Lust for Real Life* (2003) helped put the search for authenticity on the agenda as a social phenomenon. *The Tyranny of Numbers* and *The Sum of Our Discontent* (2001) predicted the backlash against the government's target culture. *Funny Money: In Search of Alternative Cash* (1999) launched the time banks movement in the UK. *Broke: Who Killed the Middle Classes?* (2013) explored the impact of recent economic upheavals on the middle classes. David also writes history books.

Andrew Simms is an influential author, political economist, and campaigner. His most recent book is *Cancel the Apocalypse: The New Path to Prosperity*. He is codirector of the New Weather Institute, assistant director of Scientists for Global Responsibility, a research associate at the Centre for Global Political Economy (University of Sussex), and a fellow of the New Economics Foundation, where he was policy director for many years. He devised Earth Overshoot Day, marking when in the year we start living beyond our ecological means, and coined the term "clone towns" to describe the urban homogenization caused by chain stores. *New Scientist* called him a "master at joined-up progressive thinking." His other books include *The New Economics*; *Do Good Lives Have to Cost the Earth?*; *Ecological Debt: Global Warming & the Wealth of Nations*; and *Eminent Corporations: The Rise and Fall of the Great British Company*. Andrew was coauthor of the original Green New Deal, published in response to the 2008 crisis, and now seen as a key policy approach for tackling climate change and making the economy sustainable. In 2018 he helped launch the Rapid Transition Alliance, an international initiative with a mission to find and spread evidence-based hope in a warming world.

ACKNOWLEDGMENTS

Because the discipline of economics is in a state of upheaval, with the certainties of the last few decades beginning to crumble, now is a fascinating time to attempt to write an introductory book about economics. Among the many others engaged in this important work are several groups, such as our colleagues at the New Economics Foundation, student-led initiatives like Rethinking Economics, and individuals working both within institutions and plowing braver and more lonely paths such as Ann Pettifor, Prof. Victoria Chick, Prof. Jayati Ghosh, Dr. Ha-Joon Chang, Prof. Steve Keen, Prof. Richard Murphy, Prof Mariana Mazzucato, Dr. Katherine Trebeck, Kate Raworth, Ruth Potts, Beth Stratford, Prof. Nick Robins, Dr. Geoff Tily, Prof. Peter Newell, and a longer list of far too many to mention.

Picture credits

The publisher would like to thank the following for permission to reproduce copyright material:

Alamy: ZUMA Press, Inc. / Alamy Stock Photo 87 (left)

Barbara Ward: Mayotte Magnus / International Institute for Environment and Development 120 (left)

Flickr: LSE Library (no known copyright restrictions on archives) 19 (left)

Herman Daly: 120 (right)

Peter Harrington Rare & First Edition Books, London: 53 (left)

Shutterstock: Kseniakrop 16 (top left), Hein Nouwens 16 (bottom left), Stock Vector 51 (top left), Vector Tradition 84 (bottom left), Everett Historical 118 (bottom left), M-vector 119 (top left), Mr. Rashad 119 (top right)

Wellcome Collection: (CC BY 4.0) 52 (right)

Wikimedia: David Shankbone (CC BY-SA 3.0) 19 (right), Pacha J. Willka (CC BY-SA 3.0) 51 (top right), Courtesy of Indiana University.doi:10.1371/journal.pbio.1001405.g001 (CC BY-SA 2.5) 85 (bottom right), photographer unknown (CC BY-SA 3.0) 86 (right), photographer unknown (CC BY SA 3.0) 87 (right), UNCTAD (CC BY SA 2.0) 121 (right)